Spiritual Writings on Mary

Other books in the
SkyLight Illuminations Series

Spiritual Writings on Mary

Annotated & Explained

Selections and Annotations by
Mary Ford-Grabowsky

Foreword by Andrew Harvey

Walking Together, Finding the Way
SKYLIGHT PATHS Publishing
Woodstock, Vermont

Spiritual Writings on Mary:
Annotated & Explained

2005 First Printing
Annotation and introductory material © 2005 by Mary Ford-Grabowsky

Library of Congress Cataloging-in-Publication Data
Spiritual writings on Mary : annotated & explained / annotations by Mary Ford-Grabowsky ; foreword by Andrew Harvey.
p. cm. — (SkyLight illuminations series)
Includes bibliographical references.
ISBN 1-59473-001-6 (pbk.)
1. Mary, Blessed Virgin, Saint—Meditations. I. Ford-Grabowsky, Mary. II. Series: SkyLight illuminations.

BT608.5.S65 2005
232.92—dc22   2005009930

10   9   8   7   6   5   4   3   2   1

Manufactured in the United States of America
Cover design: Walter C. Bumford III
Cover art: courtesy of clipart.com

> SkyLight Paths Publishing is creating a place where people of different spiritual traditions come together for challenge and inspiration, a place where we can help each other understand the mystery that lies at the heart of our existence.
>
> SkyLight Paths sees both believers and seekers as a community that increasingly transcends traditional boundaries of religion and denomination—people wanting to learn from each other, *walking together, finding the way.*

SkyLight Paths, "Walking Together, Finding the Way" and colophon are trademarks of LongHill Partners, Inc. registered in the U.S. Patent and Trademark Office.

Walking Together, Finding the Way
Published by SkyLight Paths Publishing
A Division of LongHill Partners, Inc.
Sunset Farm Offices, Route 4, P.O. Box 237
Woodstock, VT 05091
Tel: (802) 457-4000   Fax: (802) 457-4004
www.skylightpaths.com

To Axel L. Grabowsky
with infinite gratitude
for all your work on this book,
your soaring spirit,
and the love that never dies

Contents ☐

4. Mary, Source of Power and Grace

5. Mary, Mother of Us All

7. Mary, in Our Sorrow

Foreword ☐

Perhaps the single most significant mystical event of our time is the return to human consciousness, on a massive scale, of the awareness of the Motherhood of God. As an increasingly fear-driven and frenzied patriarchy degrades and destroys the world in an orgy of greed and violence, the return of the celebration of God as Mother-of-God—as the force of all-embracing divine love that lives in, for, and as the creation—offers a saving balance of reverence for the created world, an honoring of all diversity, and a new respect for feminine modes of intuition and cooperation. This revival in spiritual thinking also offers a fresh, urgent, and radical vision of love in action and a "mystical activism" that gives birth to what may well be humanity's last—and best—hope.

At the center of this return of the Mother is an astonishing revival of interest in and passion for Mary, both within Christianity and outside it. Increasingly—and for seekers of many kinds and paths—the figure of Mary is embodying all the grandeurs and powers of the complete divine Mother, of a Mother who not only governs the transcendent realms but also wills the transformation of *this* earth into the "kingdom-queendom" of which Jesus spoke continually and to which his entire mission was dedicated. The traditional limits that male theologians of the past have placed on Mary's power and significance and on her role in the Christ revelation are being shattered, and a new revelation of her role in the birth of divine humanity is being acknowledged at the very moment when the human race needs its inspiration most.

This vision of Mary as the complete and completely empowered divine Mother does not, however, deny the different truths of Mary's presence as celebrated in the Christian mystical tradition. In fact one way of experiencing the Christian mystical tradition—as Mary Ford-Grabowsky's exemplary and brilliant anthology makes clear—is as a continually self-transforming unfolding of the truth of Mary's role in the birth of Christ-consciousness, an unfolding that begins with her relatively minor role in the Gospel, expands through her growing glorification in the third and fourth century CE, explodes in the many-sided ecstatic celebration of her mystical power and glory in the late Middle Ages—in the visions of Dante, Julian of Norwich, and Hildegard of Bingen—and comes to a triumphant consummation in the work of the prophetic Marian mystic of the eighteenth century, Louis-Marie Grignon de Montfort, who declared in his *Secret of Mary:*

> It is through the Very Holy Virgin that Jesus Christ came into the world to begin with, and it is also through her that he will reign in the world.... Until now, the divine Mary had been unknown, and this is one of the reasons why Jesus Christ is hardly known as he should be. If then—as is certain—the knowledge and reign of Jesus Christ arrive in the world, it will be a necessary consequence of the knowledge and reign of the Very Holy Virgin, who birthed him into the world the first time and will make him burst out everywhere the second.... Mary is the dawn that precedes and reveals the Sun of Justice.

De Montfort's tremendous vision of Mary as a cosmic Mother-force that is indispensable and crucial to the birth of authentic Christ-consciousness in apocalyptic times has had the essential purpose of providing an expanded mystical context for the apparitions of Mary that began in the 1830s and are still continuing. Mary warns humanity of the dire consequences of continuing on its path of suicidal self-destruction and offers a way out through prayer, repentance, mutual respect, and sacred action. However hard the guard dog theologians of the Roman Catholic Church try to contain the cosmic reach and implications of the Mary of the apparitions, it is clear to anyone who studies them that *this* Mary is speaking not only to Christians and the Church, but to all beings everywhere as a universal Mother with all transcendent powers at her disposal and a burning compassion to use them for humanity's transformation and for the creation, out of the ashes of nightmarish destruction, of a new human race and a new world. The coming of the Apocalypse has called out of the depths of human memory and divine awareness an ever-richer image of Mary as the focus and conduit of an all-powerful and all-redeeming divine feminine love and knowledge dedicated to helping us preserve and transform our world.

Perhaps the most important aspect of this new vision of Mary is its insistence that this all-powerful and all-redeeming divine feminine love is, in its essential nature, radical, even revolutionary. The Mary who is emerging in humanity's mystical experience of her is not only the transcendent Queen of Heaven but also a revolutionary of love and justice, passionate for the triumph of God's Kingdom on behalf of the poor, humiliated and dispossessed, and of an increasingly ravaged Nature. She is at once the cosmic Mother of all; Maryam the Mother of Jesus, who called in the Magnificat for a triple revolution—spiritual, cultural, and political—a complete overturning of all the forces of oppression; and the Black Madonna, enraged beyond endurance at human folly, inequality and cruelty, and gifted with vast divine powers of creative destruction and sacred wrath. This composite Mary-force, known in its full majesty, outrage, and demand, unleashes a tremendous radical power that menaces all elites and hierarchies and all ways of being and acting that do not revere the harmony and dignity of life. The force of the Mother, it is becoming clear, wills, in and through Mary, nothing less than a complete upheaval of the brutal facts of the world and of all those oppressive structures that keep people and nature enslaved.

The emergence of the "complete" Mary—at once transcendent and immanent, divine and human, all-loving and revolutionary—allows, as de Montfort in the eighteenth century prophesied it would, for the birth at last of the complete and authentic Christ-consciousness, as much the child of the Mother as the Father and which is profoundly revolutionary in its intent. In the Gospel of Thomas Jesus proclaims, "He who is near to me, is near to the fire": The revelation of the divine Mary, of the Mother as both compassion and prophetic hunger to see all institutions, arts, sciences, ways of doing politics and business transformed to reflect God's love and God's justice, makes possible the birth of this "fire" on a massive scale in the world. The drama is set, at the heart of the Apocalypse, for the potential creation of a new humanity, on fire with divine wisdom, peace, power, sacred outrage, and sacred energy; and inspired and empowered to act in every dimension to preserve and transform the world. The "fire" that Jesus proclaimed the creative agent in the kingdom-queendom is not only an inward experience but also an outward way of acting. What Mary as the birthing force of this "fire" can guide the whole human race to at this moment is a new vision both of what it is to be a mystic and what it is to be an activist. Just as the historical Maryam filled in her being and life all the opposites of peace and passion, transcendent knowledge and radical embodied action, stillness and energy, so Mary the complete Mother can help birth in the human race the potentially all-transforming fire-in-action of mystical activism that fuses all the sacred powers of mystical strength, stamina, wisdom, and compassion with all the sacred passion of the Mother's vast hunger to see the world transfigured. From Mary as Divine Mother flow not only the vision of a new creation but also the birthing powers and passion necessary to bring it into being.

In 1986 Mary announced to the world at Medjugorje in Yugoslavia: "These are the times of the great return. Yes, after the time of the great suffering there will be the time of the great rebirth and all will blossom again. Humanity will again be a new garden of life and beauty." For those of us who are aware that humanity and the world are now entering the hurricane of the great suffering, this promise of a new garden by the Mother is not only a prophetic consolation but also a call to action, a call to all of us to summon up all the creative powers of our being and place them under her guidance, inspiration, and protection so that the great rebirth can, in de Montfort's phrase, "burst out everywhere."

Acknowledgments □

To Jon Sweeney, a consummate editor and a joy to work with: my deepest possible gratitude. And to the entire SkyLight Paths team, especially Lauren Seidman, Emily Wichland, Jenny Buono, Anna Chapman, and Maura Shaw: Thank you for all the hard work and individual gifts you brought to this book.

To the wonderful people at the libraries of Harvard Divinity School and Boston College, who gave me tremendous help: heartfelt thanks.

To Andrew Harvey, a luminous mystic who is willing to spend and be spent in tireless, impassioned, and unconditionally loving service to human and planetary needs in the name of Mary: thank you from the depths of my being for your magnificent contributions to this book and to my life.

To Eryk Hanut, one of the most gifted people I have ever known, a master of many arts, especially photography and writing, and a beloved friend: thank you for the beautiful writing you contributed to this book.

To Sister José Hobday, because you love Mary and never cease imitating her courage and strength; you never cease inspiring me; and blazing light never ceases pouring forth from your holy soul: thank you with all my heart.

To Sister Juan Mahan, whose love and reverence for Mary set fire to my soul and inspired a lifelong "pilgrimage with Mary": my dearest love.

To Dorothy Walters, for the support, encouragement, kindness, and generosity in your huge soul: my most loving gratefulness.

To Paola Biola, for so generously lending me books from your great Marian library and for the knowledge and wise suggestions you offered me regarding research: thank you from the depths of my heart.

To Su Skjersaa, an exceptionally gifted artist, writer, and mystic: thank you for sharing with me your inspiring doctoral project on the Black Madonna, and the beauty of your soul.

To Dr. Cullen I. K. Story and the late Dr. Donald Juel of Princeton Theological Seminary, who taught me the priceless value of studying the Christian Scriptures, of searching for the meaning of every verse, continually refreshing and updating my knowledge, and doing it all in Greek: I am infinitely grateful for the inspiring education you gave me.

To Kevin Potts, my son-in-law, for finding an extremely important article: very special thanks and very special love.

To Tara Grabowsky, my daughter, for your inspiring presence in my life, for your depths, for your example of towering courage, and for all your love: I can only thank you by being there for you with all my love.

Introduction ☐

When I was seventeen and in my first semester of college, my French teacher, Sister Juan, who was more impassioned for God and life and beauty than anyone I had ever known, was also my dorm mother. This meant she lived on my floor, and I could drop in to talk to her when I needed to. The door was always open.

One evening when I was returning from dinner with a mountain of work to do, I noticed her at her desk poring over a huge book of lush pictures, and I stopped to ask what they were about (mostly to delay studying as long as possible). She turned to invite me in, and I was startled to see the expression on her face. She looked transported. Enraptured. Like someone who has been praying for a long time and is seeing into eternity.

I sat down, and we began looking at pictures of Mary, the mother of Jesus, that took my breath away. As we slowly went through the book, pausing to talk about the images, I felt wonder rising in myself and a faint realization that something very powerful and unusual was happening. A remark from one of the mystics came to mind. It was tender and beautiful and very simple: "See how your eyes shine when you talk about divine things." And here I was, in the sight of shining blue eyes, wondering if my own looked the same, and marveling that the quiet process of getting to know Mary had drawn Sister Juan and me into such closeness with each other and with God.

For hours, we feasted on masterpieces by Botticelli, Raphael, Piero della Francesca, and Leonardo da Vinci; on twelfth-century stained glass windows from the cathedral at Chartres; ancient wooden sculptures from the Louvre; Eastern Orthodox icons; Black Madonnas; and even Madonna dolls from folk art. Mary's image appeared on silver chalices, threadbare weavings, and modern paintings by such artists as Matisse and Gauguin. Page after page of that book shone with holy light.

The evening was a revelation for me. Up until then, I had held a childish image of Mary as a passive, submissive-looking girl with downturned eyes, like the sweet little statue my mother placed on my bureau when I was born. But now my fanciful image had evolved into a picture of a flesh-and-blood Middle Eastern woman exceptionally gifted with self-confidence and courage.

With this shift in my understanding of Mary came a new curiosity about her. I soon found myself feasting on Marian literature as ravenously as I had devoured Sister Juan's book, and I have been reading and writing about Mary ever since.

This book is one of the outcomes of that memorable evening long ago. It contains some two hundred selections from throughout the world. The writings come primarily from Christianity but also from Islam and its mystical wing, Sufism. I have identified authors and annotated most of the entries to clarify difficult points. Many of the translations are my own; other translators' names are provided only in cases where I chose a non-standard translation of a common piece. The selections are arranged in nine chapters, each centering on an essential aspect of Mary's role in history and in life today.

Chapter 1, "Mary in Scripture," contains the Christian Scriptures's references to Mary and a few passages from the Hebrew Scriptures seen as prophetic of the coming Savior and his mother. The Christian Scriptures selections are arranged chronologically, beginning with the Annunciation and ending with Mary and the disciples in the Upper Room praying for the Spirit of Christ to come.

Chapter 2, "Legends about Mary," contains charming writings not found in the Christian Scriptures that seek to answer intriguing but probably unanswerable questions about the facts of the lives of Mary, Joseph, and Jesus, such as "What were Mary's parents like?" "What was her childhood like?" "What was Jesus like as a child?" "Did Mary and Joseph see signs of his spiritual powers during his childhood?"

Since there is no information in the Bible, authors filled in the blanks with imaginative stories. For example, a tale popular in the East and in Islam recounts that from the age of three, Mary was raised by priests in the temple, where she could be nourished by God in an atmosphere of holiness and scholarship. By allowing Mary entry even as a child to a sacred space usually reserved to male priests, the writer symbolically conveys Mary's holiness and extreme favor in God's sight.

Chapter 3, "Mary, Image of Our Possibilities," celebrates many ways in which Mary serves as a model all men and women can imitate. Many writers highlight her reflectiveness, for example, noting that she "ponders things in her heart" (e.g., Luke 2:41–51) before speaking and acting, as when she thoughtfully weighs God's invitation to become the mother of Christ before deciding to say yes.

Jaroslav Pelikan, a prominent Christian scholar at Yale, emphasizes Mary's universality as a model with the following comment:

> It is difficult, if not impossible, to imagine an individual life or a specific culture for which she is not an appropriate—and treasured— symbol.... She fits everywhere, and offers something to everyone.

In essence, she exemplifies the holiness that every man and woman, regardless of age or race or class, can attain.

The title of Chapter 4, "Mary, Source of Power and Grace," expresses the essence of the human relationship with the mother of God. *Life* magazine estimates that the prayer "Hail Mary" is said two billion times every day. Each year, five to ten million people make a pilgrimage to Our Lady of Guadalupe in Mexico City, while similar numbers visit hundreds of Marian pilgrimage sites all over the world. Such statistics indicate humankind's recognition and veneration of Mary's power and grace.

Chapter 5, "Mary, Mother of Us All," honors Mary as the archetype of motherhood, both in human terms and as the mother of God. Some writers in this section engage in "Mariology from below," observing the genetic similarity of Jesus and Mary, while others do "Mariology from above," celebrating the mystery of her divine motherhood. Great mystics, however, unite the heavenly with the earthly, as Dante does in the beautiful concluding cantos of *The Divine Comedy*, where he writes of the radiance of "the face that most resembles Christ's."

The sixth chapter, "Mary, Our Intercessor," shows how all over the world, for the past two thousand years, people have seen Mary as the intercessor, the advocate and helper who opens her heart to our prayers, offering men and women a reliable source of tenderness, comfort, protection, and peace.

The following section, Chapter 7, "Mary, in Our Sorrow," honors what is greatest about Mary: her ability to walk with her son on the long last day of his life through torture and execution, discounting her own agony and helplessness, with nothing but her own presence to comfort her child. Thousands of mothers of *Desaparecidos,* young men who have disappeared all over the world, murdered for protesting corrupt governmental practices, identify deeply with this aspect of Mary's suffering. So, too, do people who know loss of any kind: the end of a dream, a job, their health or youth, a relationship with a beloved. One of Mary's most fitting titles, "Our Lady of Sorrows," implies her full experience of life's hardest realities and the reason why billions of suffering men and women turn to her in prayer.

Chapter 8, "On Pilgrimage with Mary," centers on Mary's journey on earth in faith and love, as well as the spiritual connectedness that unites our own sacred pilgrimage with hers. Writers dispel the mistaken notion held by many that Mary's life was relatively stationary. On the contrary, she traveled frequently, alone or with her family, all over Palestine and into Egypt. Trips to the temple in Jerusalem to fulfill religious duties occurred at least annually; she crossed through the hill country alone to visit her cousin Elizabeth; she fled with her family, like millions of refugees today, to escape a despotic ruler's killings; and she walked the sun-baked roads of Palestine with her son—to name but part of her pilgrimage.

If we cannot follow her physical footsteps through the troubled Middle East, what we can imitate are her attitudes, which in essence pertain to faith and love. She was a dwelling place for God, and so are we.

The book closes with Chapter 9, "In Praise of Mary," which includes sacred poems, prose, chants, and songs seeking to convey the ineffable love, awe, reverence, and gratitude in the hearts of people all over the world for Mary the mother of Jesus, the mother of us all.

1

Mary in Scripture

A Prophecy

The Lord himself, therefore,
will give you a sign.
A virgin shall conceive
and bear a son,
and she shall call his name
Immanuel.
—Isaiah 7:14

This verse from the Hebrew Scriptures is considered a prophecy of Mary's motherhood. The name *Immanuel* means "God is with us."

Mary and Wisdom

The Lord begot me, the firstborn of his ways,
  the forerunner of his prodigies of long ago;
From of old I was poured forth,
  at the first, before the earth.
When there were no depths I was brought forth,
  when there were no fountains or springs of water.
    —Proverbs 8:22–24

❖ In many Christian liturgies, Wisdom texts from the Hebrew Scriptures, such as this one, are applied to Mary. According to this understanding, she holds an ultimate place in God's eternal plan as the one who will give birth to the Messiah.

Now a great sign appeared in Heaven: a woman adorned with the sun, standing on the moon, and the twelve stars upon her head for her a crown. She was pregnant, and in labor, crying aloud in the pangs of childbirth....

The woman brought a male child into the world, the son who was to rule all the nations with an iron scepter, and the child was taken straight up to God and to his throne while the woman escaped into the desert, where God had made a place of safety ready, for her to be looked after....

—Revelation 12:1–2, 5–6

❖ Rich in profound symbolism, the Book of Revelation can be interpreted on many levels. Here, the woman clothed with the sun may be seen as Mary and her child as Jesus.

I will make you enemies of each other:
you and the woman,
your offspring and her offspring.
It will crush your head
and you will strike its heel.
    —Genesis 7:14

✥ This verse from the Hebrew Scriptures is regarded as the first reference to Mary in the Bible. The context is the story of the fall: Yahweh is
punishing the serpent with a curse for tempting Eve to eat the forbidden fruit in the Garden of Eden. The serpent—a symbol of the evil
that entered into Paradise—is pitted against Mary, the "new Eve,"
whose work of serving God's purposes, which entails immense suffering, contrasts with the first woman's disregard for God's purposes when
she ate the forbidden fruit.

A Mariological Psalm

I tell of Egypt and Babylon
    among those that know the Lord.
Of Philistia, Tyre, Ethiopia:
    "This man was born there."
And of Zion they shall say:
    "One and all were born in her;
And he who has established her
    is the Most High Lord."
They shall note, when the peoples are enrolled:
    "This man was born there."
And all shall sing, in their festive dance:
    "My home is within you."
      —Psalm 87:4–7

❖ In this profound and poetic psalm, the psalmist looks forward joyfully to the time of the Messiah, when all people will belong to the People of God. Symbolically, Zion is Mary, and the entire psalm is an expression of her universal motherhood.

Shout for joy, daughter of Zion!
Israel, shout aloud!
Rejoice! Exult with all your heart,
daughter of Jerusalem!
The Lord your God is in your midst!
　　—Zephaniah 3:14–18

⌘ This reading from the Hebrew Scriptures is part of the liturgy for the
feast of the Visitation of the Blessed Virgin Mary, May 31, a celebration of Mary's visit to her cousin Elizabeth, when both women were
pregnant. Zephaniah's burst of joy suggests Elizabeth's sublime excitement when she cries out to Mary: "Of all women you are the most
blessed.... As soon as the sound of your greeting reached my ears, the
child in my womb leapt for joy" (Cf. Luke 1:39–56).

I am black but beautiful
   O daughters of Jerusalem,—
As the tents of Kedar,
   as the curtains of Salma.
Do not stare at me because I am swarthy,
   because the sun has burned me.
     —Song of Songs 1:5–6

❖ This celebrated passage from the Song of Songs is often invoked in the context of the Black Madonna, the meaning of which each century seeks anew. Statues of Mary emerged in Europe in the Middle Ages made of a single piece of wood and depicting Mary seated on a throne with the infant Jesus, looking exactly like her and seated on her lap. These statues, which were called Thrones of Wisdom, were often black and were extremely popular sites of pilgrimage, as they are today. The carving's blackness has rich symbolic value, evoking in part the mystery of God becoming human, the life-giving darkness of the womb, the dark fecundity of the earth, and wisdom.

The Annunciation

In the sixth month the angel Gabriel was sent by God to a town in Galilee called Nazareth, to a virgin betrothed to a man named Joseph, of the house of David; and the virgin's name was Mary. He went in and said to her, "Rejoice, so highly favored! The Lord is with you." She was deeply disturbed by these words, and asked herself what this greeting could mean, but the angel said to her, "Mary, do not be afraid, you have won God's favor. Listen! You are to conceive and bear a son, and you must name him Jesus. He will be great and will be called Son of the Most High. The Lord God will give him the throne of his ancestor David: he will rule over the house of Jacob forever, and his reign will have no end." Mary said to the angel, "But how can this come about, since I am a virgin?" "The Holy Spirit will come upon you," the angel answered, "and the power of the Most High will cover you with its shadow. And so the child will be holy and will be called Son of God. Know this too: your kinswoman Elizabeth has, in her old age, herself conceived a son, and she whom people called barren is now in her sixth month, for nothing is impossible to God." "I am the handmaid of the Lord," said Mary, "let what you have said be done to me." And the angel left her.

—Luke 1:26–38

This is how Jesus Christ came to be born. His mother Mary was betrothed to Joseph; but before they came to live together, she was found to be with child of the Holy Spirit. Her husband Joseph, being a man of honor and wanting to spare her publicity, decided to divorce her informally. He had made up his mind to do this when the Holy Spirit appeared to him in a dream and said, "Joseph, son of David, do not be afraid to take Mary home as your wife, because she has conceived what is in her by the Holy Spirit. She will give birth to a son and you must name him Jesus, because he is the one who is to save his people from their sins." Now all this took place to fulfill the words spoken by the Lord through the prophet:

> The virgin will conceive and give birth to a son
> and they will call him Immanuel,

a name which means "God-is-with-us."
—Matthew 1:18–24

❖ In this story, Mary's son is to be named Jesus, because he will save his people. That is, in the Aramaic language, which Jesus and Mary spoke, and in the Hebrew of the Hebrew Scriptures, the name "Jesus" and the words "he will save" are essentially the same. So the text is saying: Name him "Savior," since he will save.

Mary Ponders in Her Heart What the Shepherds Say

[T]he shepherds said to one another, let us go to Bethlehem and see this thing that has happened which the Lord has made known to us. So they hurried away and found Mary and Joseph, and the baby lying in the manger. When they saw the child they repeated what they had been told about him, and everyone who heard it was astonished at what the shepherds had to say. As for Mary, she treasured all these things and pondered them in her heart.

    —Luke 2:15–20

The Prophecy of Simeon

As the child's mother and father stood there wondering about the things that were being said about him, Simeon blessed them and said to Mary his mother, "You see this child. He is destined for the fall and for the rising of many in Israel, destined to be a sign that is rejected—and a sword will pierce your own soul, too—so that the secret thoughts of many may be laid bare."

—Luke 2:33–35

❖ Simeon's grave prophecy that a sword would pierce Mary's heart has been seen by some as a "second Annunciation." It lets Mary know that she, who is closer to Jesus than anyone else, "whose face most resembles his," will share intimately in the sorrow and pain that lies ahead for her son.

The Visit to Elizabeth

Mary set out at that time and went as quickly as she could to a town in the hill country of Judah. She went into Zechariah's house and greeted Elizabeth. Now as soon as Elizabeth heard Mary's greeting, the child leaped in her womb and Elizabeth was filled with the Holy Spirit. She gave a loud cry and said, "Of all women you are the most blessed, and blessed is the fruit of your womb. Why should I be honored with a visit from the mother of my Lord? For the moment your greeting reached my ears, the child in my womb leaped for joy. Yes, blessed is she who believed that the promise made her by the Lord would be fulfilled."

—Luke 1:39–45

✂ In this story, Mary's cousin Elizabeth calls Mary "blessed" three times, recognizing her as the mother of God, or *Theotokos*. The controversial title implies for some theologians that the one who births the one who is God must herself be divine, but others protest that Mary is the mother of God, not God the Mother.

The Magnificat

My soul proclaims the greatness of the Lord,
and my spirit exults in God my Savior
because he has looked upon his lowly handmaid.
Yes, from this day forward all generations will call me
   blessed;
for the almighty has done great things for me.
Holy is his name,
and his mercy reaches from age to age
for those who fear him.
He has shown the power of his arm,
he has routed the proud of heart.
He has pulled down princes from their thrones
and exalted the lowly.
The hungry he has filled with good things,
the rich sent empty away.
He has come to the help of Israel his servant, mindful of his
   mercy—according to the promise he made to our
   ancestors—of his mercy to Abraham and to his
   descendants forever.
   —Luke 1:46–55

❈ One of the most sacred and beautiful writings in world literature, the Magnificat became the cry of the poor in twentieth-century liberation movements throughout the world and especially in Latin America, where "Marians" took to the streets carrying her banner like a flag.

Mary and Joseph Find Their Lost Son

Every year [Jesus'] parents used to go to Jerusalem for the feast of the Passover. When he was twelve years old, they went up for the feast as usual. When they were on their way home after the feast, the boy Jesus stayed behind in Jerusalem without his parents knowing it. They assumed he was with the caravan, and it was only after a day's journey that they went to look for him among his relations and acquaintances. When they failed to find him, they went back to Jerusalem looking for him everywhere.

Three days later, they found him in the Temple, sitting among the doctors, listening to them, and asking them questions; and all those who heard him were astonished at his intelligence and his replies. They were overcome when they saw him, and his mother said to him, "My child, why have you done this to us? See how worried your father and I have been, looking for you." "Why were you looking for me?" he replied. "Did you not know that I must be busy with my Father's affairs?" But they did not understand what he meant.

He then went down with them and came to Nazareth and lived under their authority. His mother stored up all these things in her heart. And Jesus increased in wisdom, in stature, and in favor with God and men.

—Luke 2:41–52

The Wedding at Cana

There was a wedding at Cana in Galilee. The mother of
Jesus was there, and Jesus and his disciples had also been
invited. When they ran out of wine, since the wine
provided for the wedding was all finished, the mother of
Jesus said to him, "They have no wine." Jesus said, "Woman,
why turn to me? My hour has not come yet." His mother
said to the servants, "Do whatever he tells you." There were
six stone water jugs standing there, meant for the ablutions
that are customary among the Jews: each could hold twenty
or thirty gallons. Jesus said to the servants, "Fill the jars
with water," and they filled them to the brim. "Draw some
out now," he told them, "and take it to the steward." They
did this: the steward tasted the water, and it had turned into
wine. Having no idea where it came from—only the

❋ This story, which contains one of only two recorded conversations
between Mary and her son, holds vast Mariological meaning. Although
Jesus rebukes his mother for suggesting that he perform a miracle, he
promptly does what she wishes, and her intervention leads to the inau-
guration of his messianic mission and ministry with a stunning public
miracle. As Jesus' transformation of the water into wine at Cana suggests the Eucharistic mystery at the heart of the church, the story also
symbolically associates Mary with the church while illustrating her
power and effectiveness as intercessor with Christ. The last line of the
passage implies that Mary traveled with Jesus during at least part of
his public ministry.

Writer Megan McKenna comments on the symbolism of a wedding
setting as background for the miracle:

In John's gospel the wedding feast, the place where food is shared, is
a privileged place of revelation and a place of worship, liturgy, and

(continued on next page)

servants who had drawn the water knew—the steward called the bridegroom and said, "People generally serve the best first, and keep the cheaper sort till the guests have had plenty to drink; but you have kept the best wine till now."

This was the first of the signs given by Jesus: it was given at Cana in Galilee. He let his glory be seen, and the disciples believed in him. After this, he went down to Capernaum with his mother and brothers, but they stayed there only a few days.

—John 2:1–12

preaching the good news. The gift of faith is shared as surely as the food and drink. The wedding feast is the open door to the kingdom of peace and justice, the entrance used by the Messiah to come into the world. It is the place where the old promises start to become in surprising ways.

His mother and brothers now arrived, and standing outside, sent in a message asking for him. A crowd was sitting around him at the time the message was passed to him. "Your mother and brothers and sisters are outside asking for you." He replied, "Who are my mother and my brothers?" And looking around at those sitting in a circle about him, he said, "Here are my mother and my brothers. Anyone who does the will of God, that person is my brother and sister and mother."

—Mark 3:32–35

✤ Mary is seen in these verses as the mother of the Christ, whose healing and teaching work is well under way. She and her other children (or disciples referred to as "brothers") are worried about his safety, as his spiritual powers and attacks on the corrupt temple establishment are arousing stormy emotions among his enemies. Their concern provides him with an opportunity to make a point about the human family.

Many scholars today believe that Mary gave birth to other girls and boys in addition to Jesus (see Matthew 13:55b), but no conclusive evidence of that has yet been found. Jesus is believed to have been the firstborn, however.

At the Foot of the Cross

Near the cross of Jesus stood his mother and his mother's sister, Mary the wife of Clopas, and Mary of Magdala. Seeing his mother and the disciple he loved standing near her, Jesus said to his mother, "Woman, this is your son." Then to the disciple he said, "This is your mother." And from that moment the disciple made a place for her in his home.

—John 19:25–27

Waiting for the Spirit of Christ to Come

So from the Mount of Olives, as it is called, they went back
to Jerusalem, a short distance away, no more than a sabbath
walk; and when they reached the city they went to the
Upper Room where they were staying; there were Peter
and John and James and Andrew, Philip and Thomas,
Bartholomew and Matthew, James the son of Alphaeus and
Simon the Zealot, and Jude the son of James. All these
joined in continuous prayer, together with several women,
including Mary the mother of Jesus, and with his brothers.

—Acts 1:12–14

☙ This passage describes the days before Pentecost, almost seven
weeks after the crucifixion and resurrection, when the disciples gathered with Mary in a room that had been a safe haven for them to meet
with Jesus during his public ministry. The post-resurrection appearances
of Christ, which the inner circle has been experiencing for some fifty
days, have come to a close, and Christ has ascended into heaven. Now
the disciples are waiting and praying for the fulfillment of Jesus'
promise to send his Spirit on Pentecost. Mary is a tried and tested
woman in her late forties, ripened and made strong by her work of rais-
ing a son with a world-shattering destiny, and walking the harrowing
way of the cross with him. Praying with the incipient spiritual community that will become the church, she exhibits unconditional openness
and receptivity to the Divine, as she did in her youth when she said
yes to becoming the mother of the Christ.

2

Legends about Mary

A Story about Mary's Parents

When the people were going to the temple to offer sacrifice
to the Lord, among them was Joachim, a wealthy man who
always gave generously. But his offering was refused by the
priest Ruben with the explanation: "It is not proper for you
to bring an offering, as you have not begotten any offspring
in Israel." Joachim turned back in great sorrow and decided
to go to the desert to fast for forty days and forty nights,
promising himself, "I will not go back down until the Lord
God has visited me. My food and drink will be prayer."

At the same time, his wife, Anna, was at home grieving
at having no child. But the angel of the Lord appeared to
Anna in her garden and said to her: "You will conceive and
bear a child." And two messengers came to Anna to tell her,
"Your husband, Joachim, is coming with his flocks, because
an angel told him: 'Go down! For Anna, your wife, will
conceive a child.'"

When Anna saw Joachim arriving, she embraced him
and greeted him with the words: "I know that the Lord God
has richly blessed you for I, who was childless, will
conceive." And in the ninth month Anna gave birth to the
child. She asked the midwife, "To what have I given birth?"

❈ This medieval legend, which does not have a basis in Christian scriptures, nevertheless belongs to a long tradition that attributes great theological significance to Mary's role in the Christian story. She is seen as
a long-awaited child who is born through divine intervention and called
to a high destiny in the working out of God's plan for humankind.
Legenda Aurea is Latin for "Golden Legend."

(continued on next page)

and the midwife answered, "a little girl." And Anna cried out in joy: "On this day is my spirit exalted."

After purifying herself, Anna began to nurse the child at her breast, and she named her Mary.

—Jacobus de Voragine, *Legenda Aurea*

Mary as a Temple Virgin

Anna gave birth to a girl and gave her the name Mary. And when the child was three years old, Joachim and Anna decided to bring her to the temple to consecrate her to the Lord, although they feared that she might not remain there.

The priest received her, kissed her, and blessed her with the words, "The Lord has made your name great among all generations. At the end of days, the Lord will reveal in you his redemption for the sons of Israel." He placed her on the third step of the altar, the Lord God filled her with grace, and she danced for joy, and the whole house of Israel loved her.

Mary's parents went down from the temple amazed and filled with thanks and praise for God because she had not turned back with them. And Mary remained in the temple sheltered like a dove, receiving nourishment from an angel.

—Proto-Gospel of James

❖ The source of this charming legendary account of Mary's childhood is the Proto-Gospel of James, a second-century book with rich symbolic value. (The Proto-Gospel is so called because it narrates events prior to and leading up to Jesus' birth and infancy.) As essentially an account of the birth, upbringing, and young adulthood of Jesus' mother, it shows that interest in Mary was huge during the first 150 years after Christ's death and resurrection. The section quoted here emphasizes how she, from earliest childhood, was totally dedicated to God. In about the eighth century, the story gave rise to the feast of the Presentation of the Virgin in the Temple, which is celebrated on November 21.

When Mary's mother bore her, she made a vow to dedicate her daughter in the house of God and not to interfere in her upbringing in any way. So she left her in a corner of the temple. There she was found by the high priest Zechariah.... Every day, Zechariah would bring food to the child, and every day he would find the exact replica of what he was bringing her in the same corner of the temple. He asked her, "Where do you get the other food?" Mary said, "Whenever I feel hungry, I ask God, and whatever I ask for, God sends. His generosity and compassion are infinite; whoever relies wholly on God finds his help never fails."

—Jalal-ud-Din Rumi

As the mystical offshoot of Islam, Rumi's Sufi faith teaches the Muslim story of Mary's privileged upbringing by the priest Zechariah in a temple, a sacred place usually reserved for male priests. Her nourishment by God symbolizes, among other things, her radical receptivity to the Divine and her role as a vessel of divine wisdom.

Rumi (1207–1273) was the greatest Sufi mystic poet in the Persian language. He was born in Afghanistan. After his death his followers organized themselves as the Mawlawiyah order, called in the West the whirling dervishes.

Marriage Is Arranged between Mary and Joseph

And when she was 12 years old, a council of the priests said:

> Mary has become 12 years old in the temple of the
> Lord. What shall we do with her.... And they said to
> the high priest: "You preside over the altar of the
> Lord. Enter in and pray concerning her: And
> whatever the Lord reveals to you, that let us do."

And the high priest took the vestment with the twelve bells
and went into the Holy of Holies and prayed concerning
her. And an angel of the Lord appeared, and said to him:
"Zacharias, Zacharias, go forth and assemble the widowers
of the people, and let every man bring a rod, and to
whomsoever the rod shall show a sign, Mary will be his
wife." And heralds went forth over all the country round
about Judaea, and the trumpet of the Lord sounded, and all
the men ran toward it....

> And Joseph cast down his adze and ran to meet
> them, and when they were gathered together they
> went to the high priest and took their rods with

❖ This is the second-century answer of the Proto-Gospel of James to
the question "How did Mary and Joseph meet?" The author seeks to
fill in information gaps in stories circulating about Mary, Joseph, and
Jesus. The account is best understood symbolically rather than literally
as a reminder of Mary and Joseph's holiness and the divine favor shown
them by God.

(continued on next page)

them. And he took all their rods and went into the temple and prayed. And when he had finished the prayer he took the rods and went to the men and gave them to them. But Joseph received the last rod: and a dove came forth from the rod and flew upon the head of Joseph.

—Proto-Gospel of James

Commemoration of Mary in the Qur'an

[The angels said:] "O, Mary, indeed God has favored you
and made you immaculate, and chosen you from all the
women of the world. So adore your Lord, O Mary, and pay
homage and bow with those who bow in prayer."
—Qur'an 13:42–43

"O Mary, God gives you news of a thing from Him, for
rejoicing, [news of one] whose name will be Messiah, Jesus,
son of Mary, illustrious in this world and the next, and one
among the honored, who will speak to the people when in
the cradle and when in the prime of life, and will be among
the upright and doers of good."
—Qur'an 3:45–46

"How can I have a son," she said, "when no man has touched
me, nor am I sinful?" He said: "Thus will it be. Your Lord said:
'It is easy for Me' and that 'We shall make him a sign for men
and a blessing from Us.' This is a thing already decreed."
—Qur'an 19:20–21

❖ Like the gospel of Luke, these verses from the Muslim scriptures, which
were assembled from 644 to 656, celebrate Islam's version of the annunciation and virgin birth stories with extreme warmth and joy, although
Islam and Christianity differ in their interpretations of the events. Mary
is the most honored woman in Islam and the only woman to have an
entire *surah* (chapter) named for her: the nineteenth, which is one of
the longest in the book. Her son is not seen as divine, however. Today
Christianity's and Islam's mutual veneration of Mary is a strong point
where dialogue between these two great troubled faiths is possible.

A Muslim Saying

Mary said: "In the days I was pregnant with Jesus, whenever there was someone in my house speaking with me, I would hear Jesus praising God inside me. Whenever I was alone and there was no one with me, I would converse with him and he with me, while he was still in my womb."

—Abu al-Qasim ibn 'Asakir

Arabic Islamic literature from the premodern era contains several hundreds of stories and sayings about Jesus and Mary. A professor of Islamic literature, Tarif Khalidi, at the American University of Beirut, Lebanon, has called this body of literature the Muslim Gospel. Al-Qasim (d. 571/1175)* is the earliest source of the saying. Another of the Muslim tales, in which Jesus is said to speak while in his cradle, is reminiscent of this particular story and may be connected to it.

*The number preceding the slash pertains to the Islamic calendar (anno Hegirae, or AH), and the number following the slash relates to the Christian calendar (anno Domini, or AD).

From "The Muslim Gospel"

With Mary in the sanctuary was a cousin of hers called
Yusuf who served her and conversed with her from behind
a screen. He was the first to learn of her pregnancy and
was concerned and saddened by it, fearing too that he
might be thought sinful and of ill repute. So he said to her,
"Mary, can there be a plant without seed?" "Yes," she
replied. "How so?" he asked. "God," she said, "created the
first seed without a plant. But then you might say, 'If He
had not sought the aid of the seed, the matter would have
been too difficult for Him.'" "God forbid!" said Yusuf. Then
he said to her, "Can a tree grow without water or rain?"
Mary answered, "Do you not know that seeds, plants,
water, rain, and trees have a sole creator?" Then again he
asked her: "Can there be children or pregnancy without a
male?" "Yes," she answered. "How so?" he asked. "Do you
not know," she said, "that God created Adam and his wife
Eve without pregnancy, without a male and without a
mother?" "Yes," he answered, and added, "Tell me, then,

❖ The dialogue that appears here between Yusuf (Joseph) and Mary
suggests an argument made by some Islamic theologians to defend the
idea of the virgin birth, which is strongly affirmed in the Qur'an. Jesus'
unique birth is mentioned in the Qur'an: "Jesus is like Adam in the sight
of Allah. He created him of dust and then said to him: 'Be,' and he
was" (Qur'an 3:59). Regarding Jesus' death, however, Christianity
and Islam part company. Islam rejects the crucifixion and resurrection in
favor of the idea that Jesus died and will be judged like all the faithful
on the day of resurrection. In the Qur'an, Allah (God) says to him:
"Jesus, I am about to cause you to die and lift you up to Me. I shall take

(continued on next page)

what happened to you." Mary said, "God has brought me glad tidings of a word from Him, whose name is the messiah Jesus son of Mary."

—Abu al-Hajjaj al-Balawi

you away from the unbelievers and exalt your followers above them till the Day of Resurrection. Then to me you shall all return...."

Abu al-Hajjaj al-Balawi died in 604/1207.

As is mentioned above, the "Muslim Gospel" designates the vast body of Islamic literature concerned with Jesus and Mary.

The Blessing Tree

As long as Mary did not feel the pain of childbirth, she did not go toward the tree of blessings. "The pangs of childbirth drew her to the trunk of the tree." Pain took her to the tree, and the barren tree bore fruit.

—Jalal-ud-Din Rumi
Translated by Andrew Harvey

✣ The tree that Rumi has in mind here is the date palm that provided nourishment for Mary in the Qur'an's version of Jesus' birth (Qur'an 19:22–26).

Then she brought the child to her people. They exclaimed:
"O Mary, you have done a most astonishing thing! O sister
of Aaron, your father was not a wicked person, nor your
mother sinful!"
      —Qur'an 19:27–28

[Jesus'] mother was a woman of truth.
      —Qur'an 5:75

❖ According to the birth and infancy narratives in the Qur'an, when
Mary brings the newborn Jesus to show him to the people, his favored
relationship to God is immediately recognized. Awed by the miraculous
birth, they sing the praises not only of Mary but of her parents as well.

Fasting like Jesus and Mary

If you want to fast as Jesus did, he would fast all the time and lived on nothing but barley. He always wore [garments of] coarse hair, and wherever he would be at nightfall he would plant his feet and keep praying until he saw the break of dawn. He would never leave a particular place before praying two rak'as. If, however, you want to fast as his mother the Virgin did, she used to fast for two days at a time, then eat for two days.

—Abu al-Layth al-Samarqandi

�֍ The Muslim storyteller (d. 373/983) relates here legendary fasting habits of Jesus and Mary to inspire the faithful to emulate or reflect on them. It is significant that the writer pictures Jesus fasting in the Muslim manner, which underscores Islam's high regard for Jesus, not as divine but as a prophet, miracle worker, and *aya*, a sign of God's omnipotence.

One day when the child Jesus was with his parents, two angels appeared to him and to his mother. They carried the cross, the nails, the crown of thorns, and the lance—the instruments of his Passion—with which the Lord would someday be tortured and killed. This was the first announcement of the Passion of the Lord.

    —Jacobus de Voragine

❖ Chronicles like the *Legenda Aurea* by Jacobus de Voragine (c. 1228/1230–1298) have appeared throughout history, perhaps because of the longing for more information about Jesus than we have. Regrettably, virtually nothing is known about Jesus' childhood. The Christian Scriptures contains only the birth and infancy narratives and the story of Jesus in the temple at the age of twelve.

What Was Mary Like?

She was grave and dignified in all her actions. She spoke
little and only when it was necessary to do so. She listened
readily and could be addressed easily. She greeted
everyone. She was of medium height, but some say she was
slightly taller than that. She would speak to everyone
fearlessly and clearly, without laughter or agitation, and she
was especially slow to anger. Her complexion was the color
of ripe wheat, and her hair was auburn. Her eyes were
bright and keen, and light brown in color, and the pupils
were of an olive-green tint. Her eyebrows were arched and
deep black. Her nose was long, her lips were red and full,
and overflowing with the sweetness of words. Her face was
not round, but somewhat oval. Her hands were long and
her fingers also.

— Epiphanius

❖ Many scholars believe that Epiphanius, a monk who lived c. 315–403,
based his fanciful yet delightful image of Mary in part on the Shroud of
Turin, a celebrated cloth believed to contain an imprint of Jesus' face
after the crucifixion. According to their theory, Epiphanius reasoned
that if Mary were the sole parent of Jesus, then he must have closely
resembled her. Thus, the physical traits visible on the shroud could be
attributed to her as much as to her son. However, modern scientific
studies have shown that the famous Shroud of Turin dates back to only
the Middle Ages, not to the time of Christ, and its precise origins
remain unknown.

Augustine wrote c. 400 that nothing was known about Mary's
appearance. The characteristics of gravity, dignity, and silence that
Epiphanius attributes to Mary mirror the traditional vision of ideal
womanhood that she has always embodied.

If there is an apostle on whom our eyes would be fixed, as likely to teach us about the blessed virgin, it is St. John, to whom she was committed by Our Lord on the cross—with whom, as tradition goes, she lived at Ephesus till she was taken away. This anticipation is confirmed; for ... one of the earliest and fullest of our informants concerning her dignity, as being the second Eve, is Irenaeus, who came to Lyons from Asia Minor and had been taught by the immediate disciples of St. John.

—John Henry Newman

❖ John Henry Newman (1801–1890), a renowned English churchman who converted from Anglicanism to Roman Catholicism and became a cardinal, relies on the Christian Scriptures, John 19:25–27, when he says that Mary went to live with John after Jesus' death. John, the beloved disciple, stood at the foot of the cross with Mary, Mary Magdalene, and Mary the wife of Clopas when many others had run away in fear for their lives. As for his belief that Mary lived out her life in Ephesus, Newman turns to a tradition that stems from John's followers in the second century who passed on the tradition to Irenaeus (c. 120/140–200/203). Irenaeus taught the tradition to the next generation of Christians, who in turn transmitted it generation after generation to our own time.

Mary lived in a house on Mount Zion another twenty-four years after the death of her son—others say twelve years. As she reflected on this again, an angel appeared and announced her death to her, but Mary wanted to see all the apostles around her once more. And so it happened: A white cloud brought John from Ephesus, where he preached. And similar things happened with all the apostles. As they were gathered around the dying Mary, Christ appeared and told his mother that he wanted to take her home. And just as she had been without stain in her life, Mary died without suffering and her soul flew into the arms of her son.

—Jacobus de Voragine

❖ Medieval legends surrounding Mary's death—like this one from the *Legenda Aurea*, the *Golden Legend*, by the Dominican archbishop of Genoa Jacobus de Voragine (c. 1228/1230–1298)—often emphasized her direct transition into heaven without suffering as a result of her long life of love. Notice that this legend sees Mary as having lived out her life in Jerusalem, in contrast to the traditions that she went to Ephesus after Jesus' death.

How Did Mary's Life End?

St. John tells us in the Apocalypse that the dragon hastened against the woman who had brought forth the man-child, and there were given to her the wings of an eagle, and she was taken into the desert that the dragon might not seize on her. This then may well have been fulfilled in Mary. However, I do not decide nor say that she remained immortal; nor even will I vouch that she died....

Either the Blessed Virgin died and was buried, in which case she fell asleep in honour, her end was chaste purity, and the crown of virginity adorns her; or she was murdered, as it is written: 'And thy own soul a sword shall pierce' (Luke 2:35), in which case she shares the glory of the martyrs and her sacred body, which from the light of the world arose, is venerated; or she remained, for it is not impossible for God to do everything that he will. For no one knows her end.

—Epiphanius

❖ Born in Palestine to devout Christian parents who had survived persecution, Epiphanius (c. 315–403) knew from childhood that he was called to religious life, and he became a monk in an Egyptian community. Writing in the fourth century, he was struggling with a popular debate about the end of Mary's life. One long-standing tradition holds even today that she went to Ephesus to live out her life with the beloved disciple John (see John 19:26–27). Another sees her remaining in Jerusalem. In 1950, Catholicism proclaimed the doctrine of her direct assumption into heaven. Other Christian denominations and schools of thought agree with Epiphanius: "No one knows her end."

The Greatest Are Mary Magdalene, John and Mary

Where I shall be, there shall be also my twelve ministers.
But Mary Magdalene, John and the Virgin will tower over
all my disciples and all who will receive the mysteries of the
Ineffable. And they shall be on my right and on my left.
And I am they, and they are I.

—*Pistis Sophia, 193*

�֍ *Pistis Sophia* (Greek for "faith wisdom") is a Coptic Gnostic text
believed to stem from the second half of the fourth century. The author
has Jesus proclaim that his mother, the beloved disciple John, and Mary
Magdalene are sacred to Jesus. In contrast to the apostolic tradition of
the earliest Christian centuries, which excluded women from ordina-
tion, the Gnostic tradition of the same era acknowledged women's
gift for leadership.

When tomorrow,
on Judgment Day,
the cry goes out,
O Men!
The first person
to step forward will be
Mary, Jesus' mother.
       —Farid ob-Din Attar

❖ Farid ob-Din Attar (c. 1142–c. 1220) was born in what was then Persia. He became one of the greatest Muslim mystical poets and thinkers, closely connected with Sufism. He echoes Islam's veneration of Mary, seeing in her a higher level of perfection than existed in any other woman, even in Fatima, Muhammad's daughter, and Hadija and Aisha, the prophet's wives.

Jesus Welcomes Mary into Paradise

Then the angels transported her and brought her to her beloved son who was seated upon his throne; and flames of fire covered him round and about on the right hand and on the left. Then our Lord took her hand … and said to her, "Have you come, O my mother?" Then he had her ascend his glorious throne and he had her sit there with him and he told her the story of the joy and gladness which eye had never seen, and ear had never heard, and the heart of man had never imagined, that he had prepared for her.

—*The Miracles of the Blessed Virgin Mary*

❖ Legends about the annunciation, nativity, circumcision, flight to Egypt, and Jesus as a child were gathered with other material into a book named *The Miracles of the Blessed Virgin Mary* in Alexandria, Egypt, in the fourth century.

3
Mary, Image of Our Possibilities

Prayer for Spiritual Growth

Dear Lord, you see how we become used to everything. Once, we gladly took up your service with the firm intent of being wholly surrendered to you. But since every day brings nearly the same thing over and over again, it seems to us that our prayer has been circumscribed. We limit it to ourselves and to what seems necessary for just the task at hand so that in the end our spirit has assumed the size of this small task. We ask you not to allow us to narrow ourselves in this way; expand us again; bestow on us again some of the power of Mary's consent, which awaits in readiness the entire divine will, which is always as all-embracing as when it was first pronounced and which is daily conformed anew. She may have been glad or afraid or hopeful, weary of the daily work or led to the cross: always she stood before you as at first, [accepting] everything you said, hoping to do everything you wished. Behind every one of your wishes, even the smallest, she saw the great unlimited will of the Father which you, the Son, were fulfilling.

—Adrienne von Speyr

❧ Born in Switzerland in 1902, Adrienne von Speyr was one of the earliest women physicians. Married and the stepmother of her widowed husband's children, she saw over sixty patients a day, treating the poor free of charge. With the Swiss theologian Hans Urs von Balthasar, she co-founded the Secular Institute of Our Lady of the Way.

[Mary] is a genuine model to me now as she was not when I was young. As a pregnant mother and as witness to the cross, she testifies to the joy, the pain, and the promise of all human life. She unites the power of what early centuries saw in her as "male" virtue with the demanding human virtue of compassion. Above all, she reminds me of God's insistence that all creation and every human being, no matter how poor or powerless, is truly significant. How could that message be sent more pointedly than by the story of the son of God born in a stable to a poor woman? Yesterday, today, and tomorrow, the image of Mary calls on us to be strong and creative in our responses to the sacred potentialities of all life.

—Sally Cunneen

Sally Cunneen is the author of *In Search of Mary: The Woman and the Symbol* as well as several other books.

She Offers Something to Everyone

Consider the place [Mary] holds in the Koran. She is not only the most important woman in the Koran—more important than Hegar—but she receives a kind of attention as a human being that even the Prophet doesn't have. It's arguable that she's the most important person in the Koran....

It is difficult, if not impossible, to imagine an individual life or a specific culture for which she is not an appropriate—and treasured—symbol. Her devotees are a remarkably kaleidoscopic group, from Dante and Mozart to Juan Diego of Guadalupe, from empresses and queens to illiterate girls to whom she appeared at Fatima and Lourdes. She fits everywhere and offers something to everyone. Like no other figure, Mary appeals to both the emotional and the intellectual level, for she is no more than human, but blessed among women.

—Jaroslav Pelikan

❧ Jaroslav Pelikan is a distinguished professor at Yale University with a multitude of influential books to his credit.

Saying Yes

Her fruitfulness is so unlimited only because the renunciation in her assent is also boundless. She sets no conditions, she makes no reservations, she gives herself completely to her answer. Before God she forgets all caution because the boundlessness of the divine plan opens before her eyes.... In saying Yes, she has no wish, no preference, no demands which must be taken into consideration. She enters into no contract with God; she wishes only to be accepted in grace, as in grace she had been claimed by God.

—Adrienne von Speyr
    Translated by E. A. Nelson

[Mary] was the sure ground I grew in, the groundsill of my spirituality. Yet we remained comfortably at home in the bosom of Holy Mother church. My Catholic heritage and environment have been like a beautiful river flowing over my subterranean foundation in God the Mother. The two movements are not in conflict; they simply water different levels of my soul.

    —Meinrad Craighead

❖ Contemporary artist Meinrad Craighead, who for many years has been painting extraordinary images of God as Mother, found early childhood inspiration in holy cards picturing Mary that were given to her by nuns in the Catholic school she attended.

Discovering the Black Madonna

August said, "Listen to me now, Lilly. I'm going to tell you something I want you to always remember, all right?

Her face had grown serious. Intent. Her eyes did not blink.

"All right," I said, and I felt something electric slide down my spine.

"Our Lady is not some magical being out there somewhere, like a fairy godmother. She's not the statue in the parlor. She's something inside you. Do you understand what I'm telling you?"

"Our Lady is inside me," I repeated, not sure I did.

"You have a mother inside yourself. We all do. Even if we already have a mother, we still have to find this part of ourselves inside."

———————————————

Each day I visit black Mary, who looks at me with her wise face, older than old and ugly in a beautiful way. It seems the crevices run deeper into her body each time I see her, that her wooden skin ages before my eyes. I never get tired of

❖ In this compelling excerpt from the bestseller *The Secret Life of Bees*, by Sue Monk Kidd, a young girl learns from a woman of towering wisdom to let go of the despair caused by her mother's abandonment. In the heart-space once occupied by her biological mother, she finds Mary, the mother of us all.

(continued on next page)

looking at her thick arm jutting out, her fist like a bulb about to explode. She is a muscle of love, this Mary.

I feel her in unexpected moments, her Assumption into heaven happening in places inside me. She will suddenly rise, and when she does, she does not go up, up into the sky, but further and further inside me. August said she goes into the holes life has gouged out of us.

—Sue Monk Kidd

Wishing to create an image of full beauty, and to manifest clearly to humankind and to the angels the power of Divine art, God created Mary all-beautiful. In her, God brought together all the partial beauties which were distributed among other creatures, and made her the ornament of all beings, visible and invisible. Or, rather, God made a blending of all pefections—Divine, angelic, and human. She is a sublime beauty that adorns two worlds, raised up from earth to heaven, and even transcending that.

—Gregory Palamas

❖ Gregory Palamas (1296–1359) became an Orthodox monk at famed Mount Athos, Greece. He was recognized as a leading theologian of his time and particularly as a master of contemplative prayer.

She Believes

Contemplating Mary, it is easy to imagine that everything was easy and clear for her ... that she knew she was the most blessed of all women. But the Gospels do not paint this idyllic picture. Instead they present Mary journeying in the darkness of faith. Her cousin Elizabeth says it outright: "Blessed is she who trusted" (Luke 1:45). She does not understand everything that is happening (Luke 2:50). She has to accept God's mysterious ways. But she trusts (Luke 1:38). Her faith grows as she reflects and meditates (Luke 1:29, 2:19). She reflects on what the angel's greeting might mean, overcomes her initial fright, and says, *"Fiat!"* [so be it]. The Annunciation exemplifies the dynamics of Mary's faith.... She is conscious that what is growing within her womb is somehow divine. She does not doubt this interior illumination that has been granted her; she asks only how it will come about (Luke 1:34). She accepts unseen realities, and believes, because nothing is impossible for God (Luke 1:37).

—Leonardo Boff

⚜ Born in 1938, Leonardo Boff is one of the founders of liberation theology, an inspiring movement based on a vision of uniting radical social action with spirituality on behalf of the poor. He teaches that Christ held a "special option for the poor." Twice silenced by the Vatican, he left the Franciscan order to work directly for the poor in his native Brazil.

On the Assumption

The glorious virgin has ascended into heaven.... If the soul of an unborn child melted in bliss when Mary spoke, what was the joy of the citizens of heaven when they not only heard her voice but saw her face and reveled in her blessed presence among them? The whole universe is lit up by the presence of Mary, so much so that even heaven itself, irradiated with the light of her virginal brightness, takes on a new brilliance. Rightly then do praise and thanksgiving resound on high, but it might seem more fitting for us to cry rather than clap our hands! If heaven rejoices in Mary's presence, does it not follow that our world below should proportionately mourn her absence?

But let that be the end of our grieving, for here we have no abiding city: We seek the very city to which blessed Mary has gone. If we are enrolled as citizens of heaven, it is surely right for us to remember her and to share her happiness even in our exile, even here beside the waters of Babylon. Our queen has gone before us, and so glorious has

---

※ Abbot of the Cistercian monastery of Clairvaux for thirty-eight years, which came to house seven hundred monks under his spiritual leadership, Bernard (1090–1153) was called the "mellifluous doctor" because of the sweetness in his writings, especially on the Mother of God. His devotion to Mary, which shines in his masterpiece, *On Loving God*, and in his sermons, swept across Europe through some four hundred monasteries he founded. An anecdote, which follows, offers a glimpse of this great mystic's holiness:

Once when St. Bernard was traveling to a nearby town on a preaching trip, the people complained about the richly caparisoned mule he

(continued on next page)

been her entry into paradise that we, her slaves, confidently follow our mistress, crying: *Draw us after you and we shall run in the fragrance of your perfumes.* As mother of our judge and mother of mercy, she will humbly and effectively handle the affairs of our salvation.

Earth has sent a priceless gift up to heaven, so that giving and receiving within the blessed bond of friendship, the human wedded to the divine, earth to heaven, the depths to the heights.

—Bernard of Clairvaux

was riding, saying that a good monk would not ride a mule adorned so elaborately in red velvet, gold tassels, and silver bells. Bernard gently replied that he was truly sorry for the offense he had caused, but he hadn't noticed the finery.

In every mosque in the world, the *Mibrab*, or prayer niche in the eastern corner of the mosque, is dedicated to Mary. It is a shame that more Christians do not know this. Mary is the perfect woman, complete in herself, being the perfect matrix, the perfect receptacle from which Jesus could be born.

    —Shaikh Hamid

Humble Faith

From a woman ... you learn the humble faith which does not incredulously ask "why?", "wherefore?", "how is this possible?" but humbly believes like Mary and says, "Behold the handmaid of the Lord."

—Søren Kierkegaard

❖ Søren Kierkegaard (1813–1855), a Danish philosopher who is known as the father of existentialism, was also a highly regarded religious philosopher and critic of rationalism.

The Face That Most Resembles Christ's

Look now upon the face that most resembles Christ's,
for only through its brightness
can you prepare your vision to see Him.
  —Dante Alighieri

�֍ Toward the beginning of the *Divine Comedy*, it is Mary who sends Beatrice to go to Dante's aid, thus beginning the pilgrim's journey through purgatory, hell, and heaven. Toward the end of the book, in *Paradiso* 32, 85–87, the vision of Mary as Queen of Heaven prepares the pilgrim for the ultimate, ineffable vision of Christ, "the exalted son of God and Mary."

Dante was born in 1265 and died in 1321. His work resounds with ecstatic love for Mary.

Through Mary to Christ

And after [this vision of Mary], our Lord showed himself to me, and he seemed more glorified than I had seen him before, and in this I was taught that every contemplative soul to whom it is given to look and to seek will see Mary and pass on to God through contemplation. And after this teaching, simple, courteous, joyful, again and again our Lord said to me: I am he who is highest. I am he whom you love. I am he in whom you delight. I am he whom you serve. I am he for whom you long. I am he whom you desire. I am he whom you intend. I am he who is all. I am he whom Holy Church preaches and teaches to you. I am he who showed himself to you before.

I [Julian] repeat these words so that every man may accept them as our Lord intended them, according to the grace God gives him in understanding and love.

And after this our Lord brought to my mind the longing that I had for him before, and I saw that nothing hindered me but sin, and I saw that this is true of us all in general, and it seemed to me that if there had been no sin, we should have all been pure and as like our Lord as he created us....

[Jesus' words about sin] were revealed to me very tenderly, showing no kind of blame to me or to anyone

❖ Like Dante, Julian of Norwich, an English anchoress (1342–after 1416), believed that contemplatives see a joyful vision of Mary prior to the ineffable vision of the living Christ.

It is in the context of sin that she hears Jesus' tender words of consolation, which have swept the world in our time: "All shall be well, and all shall be well. All manner of thing shall be well."

(continued on next page)

who will be saved. So it would be most unkind of me to blame God or marvel at him on account of my sins, since he does not blame me for sin. So I saw how Christ has compassion on us because of sin; and just as I was before filled full of pain and compassion on account of Christ's passion, so I was now in a measure filled with compassion for all my fellow Christians, and then I saw that every kind of compassion which one has for one's fellow creatures in love is Christ in us.

    —Julian of Norwich

The Blessed Virgin Compared to the Air We Breathe

I say that we are wound
With mercy round and round
As if with air: the same
is Mary, more by name,
She, wild web, wondrous robe,
Mantles the guilty globe.
Since God has let dispense
Her prayers his providence.
Nay, more than almoner,
The sweet alms' self is her
And men are meant to share
Her life as life does air.

    If I have understood,
She holds high motherhood
Towards all our ghostly good,
And plays in grace her part
About man's beating heart,
Laying, like air's fine flood,
The deathdance in his blood;
Yet no part but what will
Be Christ our Saviour still.

※ Gerard Manley Hopkins' vast endowment of spiritual and psycho-
logical gifts first appeared in youthful journals filled with vivid obser-
vations about the emotionally exciting aspects of nature. Winds and
waves, the beauty and power of flowers and trees, lightning, winter,
and spring are experienced intensely as manifestations of God. A
slashed ash tree is felt as a personal wound. After becoming a Jesuit, he
wrote rapturous poems about Mary, like this one, where he sees her

(continued on next page)

Of her flesh he took flesh:
He does take fresh and fresh,
Though much the mystery how,
Not flesh but spirit now
And makes, O marvellous!
New Nazareths in us,
Where she shall yet conceive
Him, morning, noon, and eve;
New Bethlehems, and he born
There, evening, noon, and morn—
Bethlehem or Nazareth,
Men here may draw like breath
More Christ and baffle death;
Who, born so, comes to be
New self, and nobler me
In each one and each one
More makes, when all is done,
Both God's and Mary's Son....
　　　—Gerard Manley Hopkins

everywhere like the air we breathe. She is a sign of the ongoing work of the Holy Spirit in the soul to make humankind more noble.

The sublimity of his mystical vision of the cosmic Mary, as of the cosmic Christ, brings him to the limits of language, where he resorts to unconventional expressions and grammar. Hopkins lived from 1844 to 1889.

These growing thoughts my Mother soon perceiving
By words at times cast forth, only rejoiced,
And said to me apart: High are thy thoughts
O Son, but nourish them and let them soar
To what height sacred virtue and true worth
Can raise them, though above example high.
　　—John Milton

❖ These words are spoken by Christ in John Milton's *Paradise Regained* (1671). In this work and in *Paradise Lost*, Milton (1608–1674) sees Mary as the second Eve, who rights the wrongs of the first Eve.

You will not come to know this joyous state
if your eyes only look down at the base;
but look upon the circles, look at those
that sit in a position more remote,
until you see upon her seat the Queen
to whom this realm is subject and devoted.
　　　—Dante Alighieri

❖ These lines from the *Divine Comedy* of Dante (1265–1321), *Paradiso* 31, 112–17, refer to the vision of Mary that is provided in Paradise as a prelude to the vision of Christ.

Mary, Sister of Wisdom

O form of woman, sister of Wisdom,
how great is your glory!
For in you there rose a life unquenchable
that death shall never stifle.
Wisdom called you to make
all creatures fairer in your beauty
than they were when the world was born.

> —Hildegard of Bingen
> Translated by Barbara Newman

⚜ One of the most gifted women mystics in the Christian tradition—a theologian, visionary, poet, composer, scientist, and physician—Abbess Hildegard of Bingen (1098–1179) was rediscovered in the twentieth century. Her musical play, *Ordo Virtutum,* is being widely performed, and her chants make best-seller lists all over the world.

The Day Has Come

True God,
I will wake up today invoking your name and Holy Mary's,
for the running star has risen over Jerusalem,
and teaches me to say:

"On your feet,
all who love God,
the day has come
and the night has gone its way."
    —Folquet of Marseilles

✤ Before retiring to a Cistercian monastery, Folquet was a troubadour,
husband, father, bishop of Toulouse, and supremely cruel crusader. He
lived in the twelfth century.

Mary, Sign of Hope and Comfort

The Mother of Jesus in the glory which she possesses in body and soul in heaven is the image and beginning of the Church as it is to be perfected in the world to come (cf. 2 Pet. 3:10), a sign of certain hope and comfort to the pilgrim People of God.

> —*The Light of the Nations,* Second Vatican Council

"I am the Queen of Peace," Mary has announced again and again. Let each of us every day, offer up our whole being to her to be made into instruments of that Great Peace that she wills for the whole creation.

—Andrew Harvey

❖ Andrew Harvey is referring here to Mary's worldwide apparitions during the last century and a half, as at Banneux, Medjugorje, and Fatima. Peace and prayer are frequently central to the message that visionaries receive.

Born in India and educated at Oxford, and the author of some thirty-five books, many on the world's mystical traditions, Andrew Harvey was the youngest don in the history of All Souls College. His work has won numerous prizes and awards.

Messages from Medjugorje

I am calling you to the light which you should carry to people who are in darkness. People in darkness come daily into your lives. Give them light!

———

Peace. Peace. Peace. Be reconciled with one another.

———

Without love, you will achieve nothing.

———

If you are living the messages, you are living seeds of holiness.

———

Eliminate all anguish. Those who abandon themselves to God do not have room in their hearts for anguish.

———

Everything that you do, do with love.

❖ In 1981, six young people in Medjugorje, in the former Yugoslavia, began experiencing visions of Mary in which they saw and heard her speak simple messages of peace and love. While the nature of the apparitions remains unclear, the messages have drawn worldwide attention and inspired people all over the world to make pilgrimages to Medjugorje.

(continued on next page)

―――――――――

Pray. Pray. Pray.

―――――――――

You will discover God in everything, even in the smallest flower.

―――――――――

You will discover joy. You will discover God.

―――――――――

Act with love in the place where you live.

―――――――――

Your responsibility is to accept Divine peace, to live it, and to spread it, not through words, but through your life.

―――――――――

If you want to be happy, live a simple life.

―――――――――

What I do in you is up to you.
    —Medjugorje visionaries

The Reign of God or the Reign of the Overambitious?

The background of the Magnificat is the tragic character of a world that is unjustly ordered and therefore an obstacle to God's plan for society and for human beings. But God has willed to intervene through the Messiah and to inaugurate new relationships with all things. All Israel and all humanity yearn for this saving moment. Mary has understood: Now, in her womb, suddenly the principle and agent of salvation and liberation has sprung to human life. It is as if Jesus were already exclaiming "This is the time of fulfillment. The Reign of God is at hand!..."

Mary, too, is filled with jubilation and intones her hymn of laud and joy. Nor is her joy a kind of "whistling in the dark," fingers crossed, hoping but without a real basis for hope. No, Mary is filled with messianic exaltation. God has become the Savior (Luke 1:47), and has looked kindly upon the lowly servant woman (Luke 1:48). And behold, Mary becomes the prototype of what God intends to do for all humanity. This is why she can sing that every generation will call her blessed (Luke 1:48).

The mercy of God is not reserved for the end time alone. The mercy of God will not allow the wound to fester. The mercy of God takes historical forms, is made

Brazilian priest and liberation theologian, Leonardo Boff has poured his brilliance and the passion of a lifetime into working for human freedom from poverty and oppression. Here he contrasts Mary's awareness, expressed in the Magnificat, of God's promise of divine justice with the unbridled ambition that so often infects those in positions of power.

(continued on next page)

concrete in deeds that transform the interplay of forces. The proud, with the power in their hands, the wealthy, do not have the last word. They think they have, but the divine justice is already upon them, in history itself. They will be stripped of their power, the mask will be torn from their proud faces, and they will be sent away empty-handed (Luke 1:51–53). The Reign of God is anything but the consecration of this world's "law and order"—the decree of the overambitious. The Reign of God is precisely a protest against the "order" of this world.

—Leonardo Boff

Dearest and Holiest and Most Beloved Mother

If you still see in me something that does not belong to you
I beg you to take it out this minute
And to make yourself the absolute mistress of my being
And all its powers
And to destroy, uproot, annihilate, transmute, and
 transform
Everything in me that displeases God
And to plant in its place and make grow and make flourish
Everything that pleases you.
May the light of your faith dissipate the darkness of my
 spirit.
May your profound humility take the place of my
 arrogance.
May your sublime contemplativeness
Halt the distractions of my vagabond imagination.
May your continual vision of God fill my memory with
 Divine presence.
May the blaze of your heart's clarity
Dilate and inflame the lethargy and frigidity of my own.
May your virtues take the place of my imperfections.

⸙ Best known for his impassioned book *True Devotion to the Blessed Virgin,* Louis Grignion de Montfort (1673–1716) was a priest and mystic, born in Brittany, who dedicated himself to the veneration of Mary and care of the poor. The Daughters of Wisdom, the female branch of a missionary order he founded, thrived, while the male branch, the Company of Mary, attracted few members. His popularity diminished when the Second Vatican Council in the 1960s de-emphasized Marian mysticism in favor of a Christ-centered Marian devotion.

(continued on next page)

May your merits be my ornament and advocate before God
Dearest and holiest and most beloved Mother,
See to it that I have no other spirit but yours
To know Jesus Christ and his divine commands,
That I have no other soul but yours with which to praise
   and glorify God,
That I have no other heart but yours
To love God with a pure and ardent love like yours.

   —Louis-Marie Grignion de Montfort
      Translated by Andrew Harvey

For a sermon on the Blessed Virgin to please me ... I must see her *real* life.... They show us to her as unapproachable, but they should present her as imitable, bringing out her virtues, saying that she lived by faith just like ourselves, giving proofs of this from the Gospel.

   —Thérèsè of Lisieux

4

Mary, Source of Power and Grace

One Sunday morning, 13 May, and the feast of Pentecost, a strange incident happened. Marie, who had nursed Thérèsè during most of her illness, went out into the garden, leaving Thérèsè with Leonie who was reading by the window. Thérèsè, as usual, began her cry of "Mama, mama!" Eventually Marie came back. [Thérèsè later wrote]:

> I was quite conscious of her entering the room, but I couldn't recognize with any certainty who it was, so I went on calling "Mama" louder than usual. It was very painful to me, to have this unnatural conflict going on in my mind, and it must have been still more painful for Marie. When she found she couldn't convince me that she was really there, she knelt down by my bed, with Leonie and Celine, turned toward Our Lady's statue, and prayed for me like a mother praying for her child's life.

✤ In this text from Monica Furlong's book *Thérèsè of Lisieux*, Thérèsè's sisters, Marie and Leonie, fear she is dying of a childhood illness, but Thérèsè receives a vision of Mary that heals the wound of her mother's early death. Mary becomes her new mother.

Thérèsè was born in France in 1873 and at age fifteen entered the Carmelite convent at Lisieux, where eventually four of her five sisters would be professed. She died there in 1897 of a virulent case of tuberculosis at the age of only twenty-four, having created an original method of spiritual growth called the Little Way. While many of her contemporary religious forged rigid, self-punishing attitudes from

(continued on next page)

Thérèse, too, turned toward the statue and prayed, asking for pity from "her Mother in heaven." Suddenly she had a vision of the Virgin smiling upon her and looking at her with infinite kindness. Thérèse burst into a flood of tears and from that moment her illness was over.

— Monica Furlong

biblical passages such as "Straight is the gate and narrow the way that leads to life" (Matthew 7:14), Thérèse saw something else. For her, the "narrow way" meant a loving journey in simplicity, kindness, generosity, and unselfishness with attention to the so-called little things. Considered a saint long before her death because of her devoted practice of the Little Way, she was asked to write her autobiography, which was published the year after her death under the title *The Story of a Soul.* The book was an immediate best seller. Two thousand copies sold in a month and four thousand the next month, translations appeared rapidly, and her fame spread throughout the Western world.

Our Lady of Guadalupe

This Mary is the woman of the land. She is sister to the poor and the mother of compassion and healing for all those who live on the edges of life, walking the roads on the outskirts of the cities, living in slums, *favelas*, tenements, and the neighborhoods [where] no one ever wants to get caught having to raise their children.... She is barefoot upon the earth; her presence causes roses to bloom in December and the birds to sing wildly and the land to bring forth its seed and bread for those desperate for daily sustenance (still more than 85 percent of the earth) and freedom. She can be a spider, as in the Native American tradition, who follows a trail home bringing light to the people, silent, unnoticed, so small and so able to steal the light from those who will not share it with others. She is the symbol of the small of the earth, inconsequential except to God, found with all those who live faithfully in situations of darkness, despair, lack, and need, yet powerful in their very weakness and numbers.

—Megan McKenna

❈ The feudal appellation for Mary, "Our Lady," emerged only in the twelfth century but spread widely in the thirteenth and fourteenth centuries, becoming, under the influence of courtly love and the joyful troubadours' songs, her most popular title. Idealization of women accompanied Mary's new veneration as Our Lady. Today, thousands of Marian titles begin with this appellation; some designate locations where she is revered, like "Our Lady of Fatima" and "Our Lady of Lourdes." Others signal qualities such as "Our Lady of Perpetual Help/Peace/Love/Sorrow" and so on.

Megan McKenna is a retreat leader and spiritual director. She is the author of more than fifteen books.

Mary can be considered a mirror of the expectations of the men and women of our time. Thus, the modern woman, anxious to participate with decision-making power in the affairs of the community, will contemplate with intimate joy Mary who, taken into dialogue with God, gives her active and responsible consent, not to the solution of a contingent problem, but to that "event of world importance," as the Incarnation of the Word has been rightly called.... The modern woman will note with pleasant surprise that Mary of Nazareth, while completely devoted to the will of God, was far from being a timidly submissive woman or one whose piety was repellent to others; on the contrary, she was a woman who did not hesitate to proclaim that God vindicates the humble and the oppressed, and removes the powerful people of this world from their privileged positions (cf. Luke 1:51–53). The modern woman will recognize in Mary, who "stands out among the poor and the humble of the Lord," a woman of strength, who experienced poverty and suffering, flight and exile (cf. Matthew 2:13–23). These are the situations which cannot escape the attention of those who wish to support, with the Gospel spirit, the liberating energies of man and of society. And Mary will appear not as a mother exclusively concerned with her own Divine Son but rather as a woman whose action helped to strengthen the apostolic community's faith in Christ (cf. John 2:1–12), and whose maternal role was extended and became universal on Calvary.

—Pope Paul VI

❖ This magnificent message comes from the document *To Honor Mary*. Paul VI reigned from 1963 to 1978.

Alone of All Her Sex

She ... had no peer
Either in our first mother or in all women
Who were to come. But alone of all her sex
She pleased the Lord.
    —Caelius Sedulius
        Translated by Herbert Musurillo, S.J.

If you meet the virgin
on the road,
Invite her into your house.
She bears the word of God.
  —John of the Cross

✤   A glorious lyrical poet and one of the most illumined mystics in the Christian traditions, John of the Cross (1542–1591) wrote works of incomparable insight and beauty, such as *The Dark Night of the Soul* and *The Ascent of Mount Carmel*. If his asceticism appears inordinately severe today, it is infinitely compensated for by the exquisite delicacy of his soul and sweetness in his poetry of love. Working with Teresa of Ávila to reform the Carmelite order in Spain, he sought to restore the order to its original purity and prayerfulness.

I was seized with a feeling of familiarity with God, with Jesus, with Mary.... I wept and exulted. It was as if there were a perpetual spring of joy, of sweetness, of happy certainty welling up in me—it lasted a long while—and the memory of it has not been effaced.

—Raissa Maritain

⚜ Married to the celebrated twentieth-century philosopher Jacques Maritain, Raissa Maritain was a mystic, whose long-awaited *Raissa's Journal* won high acclaim. Here she describes an especially joyful experience of intimacy with God.

O branch,
God foresaw your flowering
On the first day of his creation.

You are the shining lily
You point before all creation
Where God fixes his gaze.
        —Hildegard of Bingen
            Translated by Barbara Newman

✤ In these images from her twelfth and thirteenth songs, the great
Rhineland mystic Hildegard of Bingen (1098–1179) conceives of Mary
as the flowering branch rooted in the "tree of Jesse," a metaphor for
Christ. She shines as the woman preordained from all eternity to give
birth to Christ.

Mary Hears and Answers Prayers

A divine power was manifested [in our church] and was helpful both in waking visions and dreams, often for the relief of many diseases and for those afflicted by some sudden transmutation in their affairs. The power was attributed to Mary, the Mother of God, the Holy Virgin, for she does manifest herself in this way.

—Sozomen

❖ This citation comes from the historian Sozomen, who wrote about AD 440. The church he mentions was built on the site of the Anastasia Chapel ("Resurrection Chapel"), a building that since the previous century had held immense symbolic importance for orthodox trinitarian Christians. There Gregory of Nazianzus (c. 330–c. 389), one of the great Cappadocian church fathers, preached orthodox trinitarianism, as established earlier in the century at the Council of Nicea. The council had opposed the Arian heresy, which denied the equality of the Father, Son, and Holy Spirit (denying, in essence, the divinity of Christ). The influence of Mary was widely credited with the defeat of the Arian cause and the final establishment, through the First Ecumenical Council of Constantinople in 381, of orthodox Byzantine Christianity.

Some evidence for the importance of Mary in this situation and in this era lies in the meaning that she apparently held for Gregory himself. In his first year in Constantinople, 379, he preached a bold sermon not only daring to call her *Theotokos* (Mother of God) in opposition to most church officials, but also declaring this title to be part of official Christianity. Gregory also broke ranks by preaching that Mary heard and answered prayers, including prayers for healing.

The Salutation of the Blessed Virgin Mary

Hail, O Lady,
    holy Queen
    Mary, holy Mother of God:
    you are the virgin made church
    and the one chosen by the most holy Father in heaven
    whom He consecrated
        with His most beloved Son
        and with the Holy Spirit the Paraclete,
        in whom there was and is
        all the fulness of grace and every good.
Hail, His Palace!
Hail, His Tabernacle!
Hail, His Home!
Hail, His Robe!
Hail, His Servant!
Hail, His Mother!
And, all you holy virtues [hail],
    which through the grace and Light of the Holy Spirit
    are poured into the hearts of the faithful
    so that from their faithless state
    you may make them faithful to God.
      —Francis of Assisi

✤ Francis of Assisi (c. 1182–1226) wrote ecstatically about Mary and was impassioned in his love for her. For him, she surpasses all women and is the model of his spiritual growth, and the model of the church as well. The earlier Middle Ages connected the figure of Mary with that of the church, but Francis' directness and clarity in the line "you are the virgin made church" is startling.

Our good Lord showed our Lady St. Mary ... to signify
the exalted wisdom and truth which were hers as she
contemplated her Creator. This wisdom and truth showed
her in contemplation how great, how exalted, how mighty,
and how good was her God. The greatness and nobility of
her contemplation of God filled her full of reverent [awe];
and with this she saw herself as so small and humble, so
simple and so poor in comparison with her God that this
reverent [awe] filled her with humility. And founded on
this, she was filled with grace and with every kind of virtue,
and she surpasses all creatures.

    —Julian of Norwich

There's another side to Mary, the Mary of the Magnificat, the prayer she uttered when (she went to visit her cousin Elizabeth). She says, "my soul magnifies the Lord, and my spirit rejoices in God my Savior." That's a prayer that talks about God bringing down the mighty from their thrones and lifting up the poor, a God of justice reaching out to the powerless.... The only place that aspect of Mary has been emphasized in recent time is in Latin America—in the so-called Latin American liberation theology.

The Mary of the Magnificat is a much more modern model, a strong woman ... who is ... interested in justice and the poor, who realizes that we have to collaborate with a just God in working for justice in the world.

    —Richard P. McBrien

�֍ Richard P. McBrien, a leading authority on Roman Catholicism, is the Crowley-O'Brien Professor of Theology at the University of Notre Dame.

Prayer to the Blessed Virgin

God paid such honor to the ark,
which was the image and type
of your sanctity,
that no one but the priests
could approach it open
or enter to behold it.
The veil separated it off,
keeping the vestibule as that of a queen.
Then what sort of veneration must we,
who are the least of creatures,
owe to you who are indeed a queen—
to you the living ark of God, the Lawgiver—
to you, the heaven that contains Him
Whom none can contain?
　　　—Methodius of Constantinople

✣ Composed in the ninth century by Methodius (d. 847), this prayer
urges veneration of Mary in two images, first as the new ark of the
covenant and second as the queen of heaven. Methodius, a monk
greatly revered in the Russian Orthodox Church, helped win a bitter
fight against iconoclasm, a movement that opposed the use of sacred
images (icons) as well as veneration of the saints and that had removed
images from the churches.

Alleluia Verse for the Virgin

Alleluia! Light
burst from your untouched
womb like a flower
on the farther side
of death. The world-tree
is blossoming. Two
realms become one.
       —Hildegard of Bingen

Let the theologians dispute about the assumption of the Madonna; that does not seem inconceivable to me, for she no longer belonged to the world.

—Søren Kierkegaard

In Jesus, we find the animating power of God's spirit made flesh through Mary and Gabriel. The life-giving breath, through which Jesus can revive the dead, is evidence of the mingling of the human and divine in the womb of his Mother, Mary.

—Ibn al-Arabi

❖ A visionary born in Spain who is known to Muslims as the Greatest Master, Ibn al-Arabi (1165–1240) embraced Sufism, the mystical wing of Islam, at the age of twenty. In his spiritual masterpiece, *The Bezels* [jewels] *of Wisdom*, he teaches the wisdom of love.

Contemporary Artists See Mary Freshly

Contemporary artists ... see Mary freshly. They challenge the rest of us to look more closely at traditional elements of faith we may take for granted or assume we understand. They ask us to see the connection between our faith and everyday life crises, pressing social problems, and even advanced scientific knowledge about human nature and the universe itself. To see, in other words, the possible eruption of the holy at any point in life, not simply in a different and higher sphere. Author Nancy Mairs, a seer whose eyes have been sharpened by her serious disability and her husband's terminal illness, sums up this attitude clearly: "God is here, and here, and here. Not an immutable entity detached from time, but a continual calling and coming into being. Not transcendence, that orgy of self-alienation beloved by the fathers, but immanence, God working out Godself in everything."

To point to this holy reality has always been the function of icons. And it has been Mary's function in particular; it is her image that has shown us the relationship of all things open to the sacred, pointing to a unity deeper than any divisions of time, reason, or race.

—Sally Cunneen

�֍ Outstanding among the authors of Marian books who published in the great era of the "return of Mary," the 1980s and 1990s, Sally Cunneen wrote *In Search of Mary: The Woman and the Symbol*, from which this selection is taken. She says that the Marian library at Dayton University in Ohio "has some four thousand slides of twentieth-century Madonnas," including some by Americans.

O, the unfathomable power of the Virgin Mother!
A woman who invaded the house of the King;
A girl—I do not know by what caresses, passions, or
    promises—
seduced, deceived, and so to speak, wounded and
    enraptured
the divine heart and ensnared the wisdom of God.
>   —Bernardino of Siena

❖ Bernardino of Siena (1380–1444) was a Franciscan theologian and
preacher of great eloquence. Appalled by the breakdown of morals, the
lawlessness, and the civil strife of the times, he attempted to instill in his
listeners a deep personalized love of Christ. Pushed to the limits of
language in an effort to express ineffable love and praise for Mary, he
resorts to the metaphor of seduction, recalling the bride and groom in
the Song of Songs—imagery that appears also in the love poetry of
John of the Cross. A profound ecclesiology and theology of wisdom
undergirds his Mariology.

Never Passive, Never Submissive

The old version of Mary as passive and submissive is a lie. Look deeply at the story and you see in it a woman of immense strength, surrendered to God but not submissive, humble, patient, tender, infinitely focused on and burning with real love but never passive. As the French mystic Meubert put it: "This virgin so tender is the most indomitable of women...." What immense strength it took to accept Gabriel's message and the long agony she knew being the mother of the chosen one would be; what fortitude and persistent courage it took to live the life that unfolded, a life of wandering, exile, danger, poverty. She had the strength to raise her son in savage circumstances (no sooner was he born than the whole family had to flee massacring soldiers) and she had the strength to let him go when he needed to wander and learn free from her, and she had the strength to accompany him throughout the agony of his death. I see her at the crucifixion not wringing her hands but *witnessing* her son's pain and standing in it, standing at the core of his and her suffering, so that as he writhes in agony and dies, she can feed him her peace, her strength, her faith, her never-failing trust. The Curé d'Ars said: "Mary is our mother twice. She gave birth to humanity twice—once at the Nativity and then again at the foot of the Cross."

—Andrew Harvey

Mary has wept! Mary has wept!… Weeping is fecund.
There has never been a sterile tear. As the rain that falls
from on high irrigates the countryside and prepares it to
receive, in all fertility, the crops and seed and fruit that will
in time come to ripeness, so it happens in the realm of the
spirit.

—Archbishop of Syracuse, Sicily

❊ This text alludes to a statue of Mary that in 1953 was said to weep
human tears.

O Woman uniquely to be wondered at,
And to be wondered at for your uniqueness,
By you the elements are renewed,
Hell is redeemed,
Demons are trampled down
And men are saved,
Even the fallen angels
Are restored to their place.
O woman full
And overflowing with grace,
Plenty flows from you
To make all creatures green again.
　　　　　—Anselm of Canterbury

�֍ Anselm of Canterbury (1033–1109), a monk at Bec in Normandy and a writer, coined the famous definition of God as "that than which no greater can be thought." In the song of praise given here, he signals Mary's role as co-redeemer, a partner with Christ in the healing and salvation of all creation.

Mary is gigantic, but also tiny and hunched with humility. Far but never, ever, distant. She is the bedside lamp that we can [reach] at any moment to dispel the darkness.

Mary draws millions to her, gives sight to the blind, makes springs gush at Banneux, Lourdes, La Salette. Mary made the sun dance at Fatima and a tree at Beauraing break into blossom in the middle of winter. She gives you what you would expect from a Queen—glory. But she also gives what you would hope from a mother. Mary cooks the soup, squinting anxiously at the clock if her child is late.

Mary is the clock, but she is also the first to forget it. Everyone knows this who kneels and prays to her. She is there; she can do anything; she has been through everything. What could be more mind-shattering than the destiny of this tiny Jewish girl, this thirteen-year-old who said "yes" to the plans of God?

Everyone knows how tremendous Mary's destiny is. That is why anyone can ask anything from her. Everyone, on one day or another, has asked her for something—even those who are closed to her mystery.

I often ask myself if the adoration we give her matters at all. She wants our best. That is all that matters to her....

A distinguished writer and photographer with a lifelong devotion to Mary, Eryk Hanut is the award-winning coauthor with Andrew Harvey of *Mary's Vineyard,* which won the Benjamin Franklin Prize. In this selection from the book, he ponders his experience of Mary's paradoxical transcendence and immanence in his lifelong, prayerful relationship with her.

(continued on next page)

Nothing is more poignant than a person who prays. To pray is to become a little child again. It is to talk to your mother without a grill between you. And the Mother listens, listens, consoles, replies....

—Eryk Hanut

The New Eve

God became man by the Virgin, in order that the
disobedience that proceeded from the serpent might
receive its destruction in the same manner in which it
received its origin. For Eve, who was a virgin and wholly
good, having conceived the word of the serpent, brought
forth disobedience and death. But the Virgin Mary received
faith and joy when the angel Gabriel announced the good
tidings to her that the Spirit of the Lord would come upon
her, and the power of the highest would overshadow her:
because of which also the Holy Thing begotten of her is
the Son of God; and she replied, "Be it unto me according
to Thy word" (Luke 1:38). And by her He has been born to
whom … so many scriptures refer.…

—Justin Martyr

This is probably the earliest extant reference to Mary as the "new
Eve." Justin Martyr (c. 100–c. 165), a great philosopher in search of a
mystical vision of God, became a Christian upon recognizing the direct
relationship between Christ and the prophecies of the Hebrew Scriptures—the "scriptures" he mentions in the text quoted here. It is
important to remember that neither the Christian scriptures nor the
institutional church existed in Justin's time. He participated in the
vibrantly living church of the first generations after Christ, when small
communities of impassioned Christians gathered at table in different
members' homes to retell the stories Jesus told, pray together, sing, and
break bread in remembrance of the Last Supper. They also took very
seriously Jesus' teaching to "tend his flock" by serving one another's
needs (John 21:15–17).

Before the birth of Mary, a constant flow of grace was
   lacking,
because this aqueduct did not exist.
   —Bernard of Clairvaux

A Vision of Mary on the Feast of the Assumption

Our Lady seemed suddenly to seize me by the hands. She told me that I was giving her great pleasure by serving the glorious St. Joseph, and promised me that my plans for the convent would be fulfilled.... Then she seemed to hang around my neck a very beautiful gold collar from which hung a cross of great value. The gold and the stones were so different from those of this world that there is no comparing them; their beauty is quite unlike anything we can imagine here. Nor can the imagination rise to any understanding of the nature of the robe, or to any conception of its whiteness. Such was the vision that the Lord pleased to send me that by comparison everything here on earth seems, so to speak, a smudge of soot.

The beauty that I saw in Our Lady was wonderful, though I could make out no particular detail, only the general shape of her face and the whiteness and amazing splendour of her robes, which was not dazzling, but quite soft.... Our Lady looked to me almost like a child. When they* had stayed with me for a little while, bringing me the greatest joy and bliss—more I believe than I had ever known before (and I wished it would last forever)—I seemed to see them ascend into the sky with a great multitude of angels.

—Teresa of Ávila

✤ Teresa of Ávila (1515–1582), a mystic, author, Doctor of the Church, and one of history's most beloved saints, founded seventeen Discalced (barefoot) Carmelite convents in her native Spain. Among her writings is the mystical classic *Interior Castle*. In her vision of Mary, images of blazing whiteness, of radiance on Mary's face and clothing, and of the unearthly beauty of shining gold and jewels symbolize the divine reality that Teresa encountered over and over again in prayer and contemplative experience.

*Joseph also appeared in the vision.

5

Mary, Mother of Us All

Mary Gives Birth to Jesus

Now at this time Caesar Augustus issued a decree for a census of the whole world to be taken. This census—the first—took place while Quirinius was governor of Syria, and everyone went to his own town to be registered. So Joseph set out from the town of Nazareth in Galilee and traveled up to Judaea, to the town of David, called Bethlehem, since he was of David's house and line, in order to be registered together with Mary, his betrothed, who was with child. While they were there, the time came for her to have her child, and she gave birth to a son, her first-born. She wrapped him in swaddling clothes, and laid him in a manger because there was no room for them at the inn. In the countryside close by there were shepherds who lived in the fields and took it in turns to watch their flocks by night. The angel of the Lord appeared to them and the glory of the Lord shone around them. They were terrified, but the angel said, "Do not be afraid. Listen, I bring you news of great joy, a joy to be shared by the whole people. Today in the town of David a savior has been born to you; he is Christ the Lord. And here is a sign for you: you will find a baby wrapped in swaddling clothes and lying in a manger. And suddenly with the angel there was a great throng of the heavenly host, praising God and singing:

Glory to God in the highest
and peace to men who enjoy his favor.

—Luke 2:1–14

Anxiety at Not Finding Her Son for Three Days

The anxiety in her heart caused her to burst into tears and sigh in deepest grief. For three whole days, she wept and moaned without resting or sleeping or eating anything. For the loss of Jesus surpassed for her the loss of anything in creation, while her love and appreciation of him exceeded anything that could be conceived by any other creature. Angels accompanied her in visible bodily form, yet they gave her no clue to find her missing boy. Moreover, during these three days, the Lord suspended all the other consolations and blessings that were usually given to this most holy soul.

—Mary of Agreda

❖ A Spanish visionary known for her four-volume work *Mystical City of God*, Abbess Mary of Agreda (1602–1665) envisions a mother's anguish on discovering that her son, supposedly traveling home with the family, has gone missing. Adding an angelic presence and the idea of withheld blessings, she conveys humankind's need to trust and persevere during times of testing.

The Visitation

And the need pressed on her now to lay her hand
   on the other body, which had gone on further.
And the women leaned to one another, and
   they touched each other on the dress and hair.
      —Rainer Maria Rilke

❖ Rainer Maria Rilke (1875–1926), the grand Austro-German poet
who is considered one of the founders and giants of modern literature, captures the intimacy of Mary's meeting with her cousin Elizabeth
when both are waiting to give birth: Elizabeth to John the Baptizer, and
Mary to Jesus.

The Motherhood of Mary

The motherhood of Mary in the order of grace continues uninterruptedly from the consent that she loyally gave at the Annunciation and which she sustained without wavering beneath the cross, until the eternal fulfillment of all the elect. Taken up to heaven, she did not lay aside this saving office, but by her manifold intercession continues to bring us the gifts of eternal salvation.... Therefore the Blessed Virgin is invoked in the Church under the titles of Advocate, Helper, Benefactress, and Mediatrix.

—*Lumen Gentium* 62, Second Vatican Council

Antiphon for the Virgin

Because it was a woman
who built a house for death
a shining girl tore it down.
So now
when you ask for blessings
seek the supreme one
in the form of a woman
surpassing all that God made,
since in her
(O tender! O blessed!)
he became one of us.

—Hildegard of Bingen

✽ Here Hildegard thinks of Mary as the new Eve, who restores what humankind's first mother lost.

He came all so stille
   There his mother was
As dew in Aprille
   That falleth on the grass.
He came all so stille
   To his mother's bower
As dew in Aprille
   That falleth on the flower.
He came all so stille
   There his mother lay
As dew in Aprille
   that falleth on the spray
Mother and maiden
   was never none but she
Well may such a Lady
   Goddes mother be.
     —English carol (fifteenth century)

The Shepherd's Hymn

Welcome, all wonders in one sight!
Eternity shut in a span!
Summer in Winter! Day in Night!
Heaven in earth, and God in man!
Great little One! whose all-embracing birth
Lifts Earth to Heaven, stoops Heaven to Earth—
    —Richard Crashaw

❖ A Puritan who converted to Catholicism, Richard Crashaw (1613–1649) was a British metaphysical poet of the Baroque era.

Letting Her Child Be Himself

We may call her the Virgin Mary, but the gospels call her the "mother of Jesus." She has the same ties with her child as any mother has. But she is also able to let go and let him fulfill his mission.

—Leonardo Boff

A Pastourelle for Mary

She is the flower,
the violet,
the full-blown rose
whose fragrance allures
and quenches longing.
More lovely than any
possible scent
is the fragrance
of the mother
of the most high Lord.
      —Gautier de Coincy

✳ For the monk Gautier de Coincy (d. 1236), as for many medieval writers, Mary is the subject of love poetry. His simple song also illustrates the tendency in the Christian mystical tradition to symbolize Mary as the mystic rose.

The Maternal Face of God

The tradition of our faith has concentrated its entire feminine content in Mary, the mother of Jesus. The whole numinous, luminous potential of the feminine is made concrete in her, so that we see her as "Our Lady," virgin, mother, wife, widow, queen, wisdom, God's tabernacle, and so on. But the feminine has almost never been regarded as a way to God. In Christian culture as we have it, the idea that God is our mother goes against the grain. And yet, if we mean to take the emergence of the feminine in our culture as seriously as it deserves to be taken, we cannot evade this issue. Is it not a sign for Western culture that Pope John Paul I could state, in public audience, that while God is indeed our Father, God is our Mother even more?

—Leonardo Boff

❖ The Brazilian priest Leonardo Boff became well known in the 1980s for his teaching of liberation theology and for his activist leadership in the movement to liberate the poor in Latin America. In his book *The Maternal Face of God,* from which these passages are taken, he looks at teachings about Mary in light of the need for women to participate fully in life.

The Face That Most Resembles Christ's

Mary was no mere instrument in God's dispensation. The Word of God ... did not merely pass through her, as He may pass through us in Holy Communion. It was no heavenly body which the Eternal Son assumed.... No, he imbibed, he sucked up her blood and her substance into His Divine Person. He became man from her, and received her lineaments and her features as the appearance and character under which He should manifest Himself to the world. He was known, doubtless, by his likeness to her, to be her Son.... Was it not fitting ... that the Eternal Father should prepare her for this ministration by some preeminent sanctification.

—John Henry Newman

❖ The title "The Face That Most Resembles Christ's" comes from the concluding cantos of Dante's *Divine Comedy*.

If you fear the Father,
go to the Son;
if you fear the Son,
go to the Mother
—Bernard of Clairvaux

Mary is called Mother. And when is Mary not a mother? "The gathering together of the waters he called seas (maria)" (Genesis 1:10). Was it not she who conceived in her single womb the people going out of Egypt, that Egypt might come forth as a heavenly progeny reborn to a new creation, according to the words of the Apostle: "Our fathers were all under the cloud, and all passed through the sea. And all in Moses were baptized, in the cloud, and in the sea"? That Mary might always lead the way in humanity's salvation, in her own right, she went with a canticle before that same people, whom the generating waters had brought forth to light.

—Peter Chrysologus

◈ In the middle of the fifth century, when Peter Chrysologus, Archbishop of Ravenna, wrote these words in a sermon, some people believed that Mary had lived through other incarnations on earth, and traces of the belief are found in Chrysologus' works. For example, he sees Mary as the very waters of the Red Sea, which parted when the Jews escaped their enslavement in Egypt. She is also Miriam, who sings a triumphal song (canticle) after the successful crossing (Exodus 15:19–21). Much later, Celts understood Brigid as another incarnation of Mary. A pronouncement against reincarnation, issued in 553, gradually dispelled the idea.

The Black Madonna

She is the Black Madonna, her face slashed in violence and rage, who sees and is witness to all the horror men and women are capable of inflicting upon one another in war, murder, torture. She is caught up with the civilians of all nations eating one another alive, sending thousands into exile, driving the weakest of the earth into fear and insecurity, while the earth is pillaged and left a desolate, uninhabitable wasteland. In Asian countries, she is called Kuan Yin, or Kannon, "the one who hears all cries," and with many arms she reaches out in pity and compassion to all seeking help, listening to the sorrows of the world. As one Japanese poet said, "She is a mother. She has born a child in the midst of tenderness and violence. And I remember that whenever I look at my own wife and child, conscious of their own fragility and indescribable beauty. And she becomes every woman, child, and man who hopes for a just life."

—Megan McKenna

In you the Lord placed his tabernacle and was pleased to be contained in you.

In me the Lord took up his abode, that I might restore the dignity of women.

    —*Questions of Bartholomew*

✣ Mary plays a central role in the ancient manuscript known as the *Questions of Bartholomew*, which was related to the lost *Gospel of Bartholomew*, a document popular in the third century.

A Bridge to Islam

When the prophet scoured out all of the graven images in the Ka'aba in Mecca He left the image of the virgin and child. And one of his last and most mysterious sayings was: Paradise is at the feet of the mothers. Mary could be the place where Islam and Christianity might meet. The hearts of the two faiths could be united.

—Andrew Harvey

In the center of the Christian story stands not the "lovely white lady" of artistic and popular imagination, kneeling in adoration before her son. Rather it is the young pregnant woman, living in occupied territory and struggling against victimization and for survival and dignity.

    —Elizabeth Schussler Fiorenza

✤ In contrast to Dante's lyrical depiction of Mary as Queen of Heaven, Harvard Divinity School professor Elizabeth Schussler Fiorenza puts forth an image of Mary as totally human, a poor village girl who "had problems with her difficult son associating with disreputable people." From this perspective the idea of Mary's perpetual virginity may be seen as a symbol of independence, autonomy, and integrity, preventing submission to other people.

Mary's Way

It is the way of the example of the virgin of Nazareth, a woman of faith, of silence, of attentive listening. It is also the way of a Marian devotion inspired by knowledge of the inseparable bond between Christ and his Blessed Mother; the mysteries of Christ are also in some sense the mysteries of his Mother, even when they do not involve her directly, for she lives from him and through him. By making our own the words of the Angel Gabriel and Saint Elizabeth contained in the Hail Mary, we find ourselves constantly drawn to seek out afresh in Mary, in her arms and in her heart, the "blessed fruit of her womb."

—Pope John Paul II

This selection is taken from John Paul II's apostolic letter "On the Most Holy Rosary."

Long before Mary had conceived Jesus in her womb,
she had conceived him in her mind and heart.
   —Augustine of Hippo

❊ Augustine of Hippo (354–430) implies that from the time of the
Annunciation, when Mary agreed to be the mother of Christ, the mystery of redemption was taking form in her mind and she was ponder-
ing it in her heart, just as she would later ponder other great mysteries,
such as her twelve-year-old son's precocious conversation with schol-
arly rabbis (John 21:15–17).

To Mary

O most resplendent jewel
unclouded by the brilliance
of sunlight streaming through you!
You are a leaping fountain
flowing from the Father's heart....
Mother of the Word
through which God created
the first matrix of the world,
which Eve threw into chaos.
Through you the Father
fashioned this Word as man.
You are the luminous matrix
through which the Word
breathed forth all virtues,
as in the primal matrix
it breathed into being
all that is.
                —Hildegard of Bingen

❖ In Hildegard's mystical vision of the Mother of God, Mary is the
"luminous matrix" of the new world. That is, her motherhood of Christ
brings into being a better world than the old world damaged in Paradise. A complex theology of the Word is fundamental to her vision.

This day the Eden of the New Adam welcomes its living Paradise, in whom our sentence has been repealed.... Eve heeded the message of the serpent ... and together with Adam was condemned to death and assigned to the world of darkness.

But how could death swallow this truly blessed soul, who humbly heeded the word of God?... How could corruption dare to touch the body that contained Life itself? The very thought is abhorrent, repugnant, in regard to the body and soul of the Mother of God.

—John of Damascus

❈ In his forties, John of Damascus (c. 675–c. 749) gave away his considerable wealth to relatives, the poor, and the church and became a monk of St. Sabas in Jerusalem, where each man lived in absolute solitude, joining the community only during liturgies. He devoted himself to writing and became an influential theologian. In the short passage quoted above, he defends the Assumption, which was officially proclaimed only in 1950. (The "new Adam" is Christ, even as Mary is the "new Eve.")

The Mystery of Mary

She is our Mother.
But she is also our daughter.
A little girl and the Queen of Heaven.
The Queen of the Angels—
and yet she is still a little girl!
Remember this!
  —Georges Bernanos

�֍ Georges Bernanos was a twentieth-century French novelist best known for his novel *The Diary of a Country Priest.*

Mary, Mother of Love

Whatever gifts God bestowed upon us
There was no one who could
Understand true love
Until Mary, in her goodness,
And with deep humility,
Received the gift of Love.
She it was who tamed wild Love
And gave us a lamb for a lion;
Through her a light shone in the darkness
That had endured for so long.
        —Hadewijch

❖ A master of mystical love poetry in the mid-thirteenth century, the Dutch nun Hadewijch was powerful in the Beguine movement, which flourished in European countries from the twelfth to the fourteenth centuries and has been called Europe's first women's movement. The Beguines lived in communities and embraced the Christian life of prayer and love (in the form of service) with great devotion, but without taking religious vows. Men who embraced this lifestyle were called Beghards. Hadewijch's work was lost until the nineteenth century, when scholars came across it in two small bundles in a Brussels attic.

6

Mary, Our Intercessor

Tale of the Bindweed

One day a driver got stuck with his wagon, which was heavily loaded with wine. He could not budge from the spot. The Mother of God of the Road came along and saw that the poor man was in trouble and spoke to him: "I am tired and thirsty; give me a glass of wine." The driver answered, "Gladly, but I have no glass in which to pour the wine for you." Then the Mother of God broke off a small white flower with red stripes. The driver filled the blossom with wine and the Mother of God drank it. At that moment the wagon came free and the driver could continue his journey. And to this day the flower is called "the little glass of the Mother of God."

—The Brothers Grimm

❊ This enchanting tale suggests, among other things, the divine love that wants to be poured out into the world through Mary's intercession. The blossom of the bindweed is selected because it notably resembles the cup of a wineglass.

The Grimm brothers, Jakob (1785–1863) and Wilhelm (1786–1859), are famous for their classic collection of folk songs and folktales, which led to the science of folklore. Jakob was also a renowned historical linguist and German philologist.

I pray to the Divine Mother of God,
Heavenly Queen of all living things,
That she may grace me the pure light of the tiny animals
That have a single letter in their vocabulary.
      —Federico García Lorca
        Translated by Andrew Harvey

Words to Juan Diego

Hear me, my littlest son: Let nothing discourage you, nothing depress you. Let nothing alter your heart or your countenance. Do not fear any illness, anxiety or pain. Am I not your mother? Are you not under the protection of my mantle? Am I not your fountain of life? Is there anything else that you need?

—Our Lady of Guadalupe

On December 12, 1531, a poor Mexican named Juan Diego climbed a hill that is today the heart of Mexico City and the site of the great Basilica of Guadalupe. There he had a vision of Mary asking him to deliver a message to the bishop: she wanted a shrine built where all people could pray. Her image appeared on Juan Diego's *tilma* (cloak), which convinced the bishop that the apparition was genuine. Today the cloak is displayed in the Basilica and is visited by five to ten million people each year.

A Prophetic Dream

I had a dream of a beautiful place where a man was dressed all in white. His robes were long like those in which we see the apostles portrayed, and he made a gesture beckoning us to go in a certain direction. We arrived at our destination, and I entered it with a companion. It was a very beautiful place with no covering overhead but the sky. It was very silent there, and that was part of the beauty. On my right there was a little church constructed of white marble in an attractive, ancient style. At the top of the pinnacle the Blessed Mother was seated on a chair holding her little Jesus in her lap with her arms around him. It was very elevated there, and below, spreading all around, was a vast country with many mountains and valleys and a thick fog. The Mother of God, the Blessed Virgin, looked out at this country and what she saw awakened as much compassion as fear in her heart. I ran toward the Divine Mother, holding

---

⟨❖⟩ Born to a family of bakers in Tours, France, Marie Guyart (Marie of the Incarnation) (1599–1672) was widowed at about the age of nineteen, and some twelve years later entered the Ursuline order, leaving her distraught son with relatives. It was a time of French missionary activity in Canada, and Marie was invited by Jesuit missionaries to make the arduous three-month-long ocean voyage to Canada, where she would minister to Indians in Quebec. Her uncanny dream related above seems to have prefigured the journey and given her the sense of adventure, excitement, and courage to undertake the harrowing change of lifestyle. Marie's sense of being protected by the grace of Mary would sustain her in the years of ordeal and hardship that would follow. Perhaps the "thick fog" in her prophetic dream symbolized the

(continued on next page)

out my arms to touch this little church on which she was seated. I felt that she was speaking to Jesus of this country and of me and that she had some plan for me. She turned toward me, and with endearing grace and a smile full of love, kissed me without saying a word.

—Marie Guyart

soul-darkness she would go through in adjusting to freezing weather, intense poverty, wars between converted and unconverted tribes, arson, and other trials. But her devotion to Mary, her strong prayer life, and her unconditional dedication to the people she served led her to give her all, and after her death, she was beatified. Blessed Marie of the Incarnation has not yet been canonized.

The art most appropriate to the Blessed Virgin Mary is the painter's. By a sure instinct, this relationship was grasped at the outset: hence the tradition that St. Luke painted a portrait of the Virgin. Sculpture cannot render what is so important in a woman, vivacity of expression. But the sculptor has one advantage over the painter: from a single block of stone he can draw forth a group—a Mother and Child. And the smooth curves of ivory made a perfect medium for the promise and innocent hope of childhood. Perhaps surprisingly, architecture seems to be the art most powerfully inspired by the Blessed Virgin. Already in pagan times the Parthenon had been dedicated to the Virgin Athene. After the sixth century, it was turned into a Christian Church of the *Theotokos*; as if purity were best translated by mere proportion.

    —Jean Guitton

❖ Jean Guitton, a twentieth-century French Catholic layman, authored the book *The Blessed Virgin* (1949), in which this selection is found. More than two decades before the Second Vatican Council sought to improve ecumenical relationships, Guitton honored the belief held by many Protestants that while there is a special quality to Mary's motherhood, there is a region reserved for God alone into which Mariologists must not intrude. He dedicated the book in part to "Protestants, Anglicans, and Orthodox."

Holy Virgin of virgins,
Mother of good counsel,
Virgin most wise,
Mother most pure,
Virgin most faithful,
Pray for us.

—From a Litany of Loreto, Italy

Prayer to Mary in Her Title of
La Conquistadora (Conqueror)

O Maria Conquistadora, promised in Eden as the woman whose seed would crush the serpent's head, help us to conquer evil in our midst, and in our hearts, with the grace of your Son Jesus Christ, Our God....

O Maria Conquistadora, through Jesus who is the prince of peace and universal king, convert by his Divine power, which is beyond all human power ... the enemies of his peace.

O Maria Conquistadora, do conquer our hearts with your pure loveliness, so that drawn from the way of sin to the teachings of your son, we will honor him in this life and victoriously come to know him, with you and all the saints forever in the next.

 —Source unknown

❖ In this powerful prayer, the Spanish word *conquistadora* is the singular feminine form of *conquistadore*, which designates Cortez and members of the army he used to brutally conquer Mexico between 1519 and 1521, destroying its flourishing indigenous civilization. The anonymous author wisely transfers the *conquistadores'* power to Mary, implying the ideal transformation of humankind's destructive force into the power of love, peace, and goodness.

Intemerata Dei Mater

No peace can last without you,
no hope for any work can be fulfilled without you;
no safety for our homes can remain or for our world,
no shelter for any of our possessions of which
you, O Queen, are the most precious.
Mother of God,
watch always over all things and,
with a glad smile,
embolden the just,
feed them your sweet honey,
seat them at all moments
at the Feast of God.

> —Adapted by Andrew Harvey
>   from a medieval hymn;
>   editor's versification

And this is the way of Guadalupe:
Do listen to me, my littlest ones;
I want a shrine in your heart where I will reveal myself;
I will come down from above
And here I will reveal myself to you.

    —Anonymous

❧ In this *salve* from sixteenth-century Mexico, Our Lady of Guadalupe brings the poorest of the poor a message of salvation.

Lord, send your dew upon this sterile earth,
and it will return to life.

At the feet of my mother, Mary,
I come back to life.
All you that suffer,
come to her.
All you that work in this house of God,
Mary knows your labors and counts your steps.
Tell yourselves:
At the feet of Mary, I come back to life.
You that dwell in this monastery,
let go of material things.
Your life and your salvation are at Mary's feet.
I dwell in my mother's heart,
there I find the One I love.
In the heart of Mary
I have found life.
Do not say I am an orphan.

❊ The author of these unusual verses was a Lebanese Arab Christian nun born in Galilee in 1846. Her mother, after giving birth to twelve sons, all of whom died in infancy, made a pilgrimage on foot to Bethlehem to implore Mary for a girl, and the following year Mariam was born. Although Mariam remained illiterate throughout her life and had to dictate her verse to others, she revealed prodigious mystical gifts, received the stigmata (mysterious appearance of wounds resembling those of Christ), and became famous in her time. She died in 1878 and was beatified (especially honored by the Catholic Church) in 1983.

(continued on next page)

I have Mary for my mother, my father is God.
The serpent, the dragon, wished to take my life;
But at the feet of Mary, I recovered my life.
She called me to this monastery, and here
will I forever remain.
At the feet of Mary, I came to life again.

—Mariam Baouardy

There in the love of Jesus is your help. Love is so powerful it makes everything ordinary. So love Jesus, and everything that he has is yours. By his Godhood, he is the maker and giver of time. By his manhood, he is truly the keeper of time. And by his Godhood and manhood together he is the truest accountant of the spending of time. Knit yourself, then, to him by love and by faith. And in virtue of that knot, you shall be a regular partner with him and with all who are so well fastened to him by love: that is, with our Lady, Saint Mary, who was full of all grace in the keeping of time, and with all the angels of heaven that can never lose time, and with all the saints in heaven and on earth, who by the grace of Jesus keep time in perfect justice because of love.

—Anonymous

❖ A jewel in Christian contemplative literature, *The Cloud of Unknowing* was written by an anonymous fourteenth-century monk in England who was a consummate spiritual director. Having learned through his own rich practice of contemplation (fifteen minutes morning, noon, and night, and a half hour after vespers) that thought can never penetrate the "cloud of unknowing," the veil between God and humankind, he taught that the one certain way to God in this life is love. His method of contemplative prayer creates "fellowship with Mary" as well as with Jesus.

This day Mary has become for us
the heaven that births God,
for in her the exalted Godhead
has descended and dwelled;
in her has He grown small,
to make us great.
    —Ephrem of Syria

Ephrem of Syria (306–373), the head of a cathedral school, composed hundreds of hymns during his last ten years as a monk, during which time he was living in a cave. Some five hundred are extant, many in praise of Mary, like the beautiful song reprinted here.

To Our Lady of Liberation

O Mary, Mother of Christ and of the People of God, we prepare for our evangelical mission. We must continue it, increase it, and perfect it. And so we turn our thoughts to you. We think of you in a special way because of that perfect model of thanksgiving, the hymn you sang when your cousin, Elizabeth, mother of John the Baptist, called you blessed among women. You did not become complacent in your blessedness, but directed your thoughts to all of humanity. Yes, you thought of everyone, but you had a special preference for the poor, the same preference that your Son would have one day. What is it in you—in your words, in your voice, when you proclaim in your Magnificat the humbling of the arrogant and the exaltation of the humble, the satisfaction of the starving, and the dismay of the rich—what is it in you that no one dares to call a revolutionary, or to look at *you* with suspicion? Lend us your voice! Sing with us! Beg your Son to accomplish in us, in all their fulness, his Father's plans.

—Dom Helder Camera

❖ A visionary Brazilian bishop, poet, and social activist, Dom Helder Camera died in 2000 at the age of ninety. He called on the church to work for social change and the empowerment of the poor, emphasizing, like Leonardo Boff and other liberation theologians, a "special preference for the poor" as the heart of the gospel message.

A Celtic Prayer to the Virgin

The Virgin was seen coming, the young Christ at Her breast, angels bowing in submission before Them, and the King of the Universe saying it was fitting.

The Virgin of ringlets most excellent, Jesus more surpassing white than snow, melodious Seraphs singing Their praise, and the King of the Universe saying it was fitting.

Mary, Mother of Miracles, help us, help us with Thy strength: bless the food, bless the board, bless the ear, the corn, and the victuals.

The Virgin most excellent of face, Jesus more surpassing white than snow, She like the moon rising over the hills, He like the sun on the peaks of the mountains.
— Traditional folk prayer from Scotland

❖ Notice that in this traditional folk prayer, which may also have been a song, Mary is compared to the moon, a primordial symbol of the feminine, while Jesus is associated with the sun, which is archetypically seen as masculine. These two images of Mary and Jesus appear throughout Christian literature.

Prayer to Our Lady of Cumbermere

O Mary, you desire so much to see Jesus loved. Since you love me, this is the favor which I ask of you: to obtain for me a great personal love of Jesus Christ. You obtain from your Son whatever you please; pray then for me that I may never lose the grace of God, that I may increase in holiness and perfection from day to day, and that I may faithfully and nobly fulfill the great calling in life which your Divine Son has given me. By that grief which you suffered at Calvary when you beheld Jesus dying on the Cross, obtain for me a happy death, that by loving Jesus and you, my Mother, on earth, I may share your joy in loving and blessing the Father, the Son and the Holy Spirit forever in Heaven. Amen.

Our Lady of Cumbermere,
pray for us.
—Madonna House Apostolate

✼ Cumbermere, a village in Ontario, Canada, is where Catherine de Hueck Dougherty, in 1947, founded an apostolate named Madonna House. The members comprise some two hundred Roman Catholic lay people and clergy dedicated to prayer, justice, work, and serving Christ. Twenty field houses carry out the global ministry. Formal veneration of Our Lady of Cumbermere began in 1960, when a statue of Mary, sculpted by the California artist Frances Rich, was installed in an outdoor shrine and officially blessed.

Prayer to Our Lady of Lourdes for Health

As we call to mind the apparitions of Mary,
May we be given increased health
Of mind and body,
Through the same Jesus Christ,
Mary's son,
Who lives and reigns with you
And the Holy Spirit, one God,
World without end. Amen

—Source unknown

Memorare

Remember, O most gracious Virgin Mary, that never was it known that anyone who fled to your protection, implored your help, and sought your intercession, was left unaided. Inspired by this confidence, I fly to you, O Virgin of Virgins, my Mother; to you I come; before you I stand sinful and sorrowful. O Mother of the Word Incarnate, despise not my petitions, but in thy mercy hear and answer me. Amen.

—Bernard of Clairvaux

7

Mary, in Our Sorrow

Lament of Mary

I am overwhelmed, O my son,
I am overwhelmed by love
And I cannot endure
That I should be in the chamber
And you on the wood of the cross;
I in the house
And you in the tomb.
     —Romanos Melodos

�֍ This exquisite *kontakion* belongs to the well-known stream of Christian literature written about the *Mater Dolorosa*, the grieving mother
lamenting the loss of her arrested, tortured, and executed child.
   Romanos Melodos (first half sixth century) introduced the *kontakion*,
a Byzantine poetic form important in liturgical music, into Byzantine
religious practice. He came from Syria.

Mama,
why have you come?
You cause me a mortal wound,
for your weeping pierces me
like the sharpest sword.

Son, pale and ruddy
Son without compare:
Son, on whom will I rely?
Son, why are you abandoning me?
Son, pale and white,
Son of the laughing face,
Son, why has the world,
O my son, so hated you?
                —Jacopone da Todi

�֎   This masterpiece, a powerfully poignant meditation on the Passion of
Christ, was written by a Franciscan spiritual genius, Jacopone da Todi
(c. 1230–1306).

Sorrow for my Beloved's sake
is a treasure in my heart;
my heart is "Light upon Light,"
a beautiful Mary with Jesus in its womb.
     —Jalal-ud-Din Rumi

The Mother of God

The threefold terror of love; a fallen flare
through the hollow of an ear;
Wings beating about the room;
The terror of all terrors that I bore
The heavens in my womb …
What is this flesh I purchased with my pains,
This fallen star my milk sustains,
This love that makes my heart's blood stop
Or strikes a sudden chill into my bones
And bids my hair stand up?
        —William Butler Yeats

※ The Irish poet William Butler Yeats (1865–1939) won the Nobel Prize
for literature in 1923.

Where has he gone,
My dearest Son?
Perhaps during the uprising
The cruel enemy killed him.
           —Henryk Gorecki

❖ These lines from the Third Symphony of composer Henryk Gorecki
   enlarge the theme of Mary's sorrow over the loss of Jesus to include
   mothers of men killed in World War II and, by extension, all who die
   in wars and revolutions—today more than ever.

At the Manger Mary Sings

Sleep. What have you earned from the womb that bore you
But an anxiety your Father cannot feel? Sleep.
What will the flesh that I gave do for you,
Or my mother love, but tempt you from His will?
Why was I chosen to teach His son to weep?
    Little One, sleep.
      —W. H. Auden

❖ Among the works of the English poet and man of letters W. H. Auden (1907–1973) are many lovely religious poems.

Christ and His Mother at the Cross

Christ:
Mother, take my broken heart
For your own to share apart.
John, beloved as you are
Shall be to you a son.

John, my mother here behold;
Take her tenderly and hold
her in your love. For she is cold,
her heart has come undone.

Mary:
Son, your spirit has gone forth.
Son of all surpassing worth.
My eyes are in their vision dark
And dying is my heart.

Hear me, Son, so innocent,
Son of light magnificent
Spending and now spent,
and only darkness for my part.
Son of whiteness and of rose,
Son unrivaled as the snows,

❖ A lawyer who joined the Franciscans, Jacopone da Todi
(c. 1230–1306) became a Christian mystic of the finest kind, writing
rapturous poetry and "spiritual songs" that were widely influential. The
"sword" that Mary feels as her son dies is that prophesied by Simeon
in Luke 2:33–35.

(continued on next page)

Son my bosom held so close,
My heart, why have you gone?

John, disciple whom he loved,
your brother must be dead,
for I feel the sword through me
as prophesied.

     —Jacopone da Todi

May I ponder in my mind,
my crucified God,
who died for me,
and experience in my heart
that compassion
that your innocent mother
and Mary Magdalene felt
at the actual hour of your passion.
　　　—Bonaventure

※ The guiding light of the Franciscans after the death of Francis,
Bonaventure (1221–1274), a theologian with immense intellectual gifts
who taught that the purpose of knowledge is love, is called the Angelic
Doctor (the Seraphic Doctor). The title relates to his vision of a six-
winged seraph (angel) that deepened his understanding of the mystical
journey to and in God through purification, illumination, and union.

A Latin American Hail Mary

Ave Maria, of the third world, full of grace, all you who know pain, know the anxieties and the subhuman condition of your people, the Lord is with you, with all who suffer, who hunger and thirst for justice, who know neither letters nor figures.

Blessed are you among women, the women and men of the roads and pueblos, of furrowed faces, of brawny muscles, of calloused hands, of forlorn eyes, but with hope.

Blessed is the fruit of your womb, Jesus. Because without him, our life and the struggle for human dignity has no meaning.

Sancta Maria, all of you holy, a thousand times holy, by your lives, by the times [that] you carry water, that you smudge your face at the hearth, trusting and hoping in God. He has made you Mother of God.

Pray for us sinners, for it is our fault, in one way or another, by our egoism and envy, that you, joined with the rest of the women and the men of the poor, the third world, suffer misery, totalitarian governments, economic repression, wars and blood and hatred.

Now, so that we change, so that there will be a conversion of heart and of all men and women towards your Son, our brother.

And at the hour of our death, so that the Lord have mercy on all who have offended him in our brothers and our sisters, in the men and women of a world that is struggling desperately for life. Amen.

—Source unknown

This poignant prayer was written down from an oral tradition by Fr. Jose Antonio Esquivel, S.J.

Yes, all honour to her! O, God, when the message comes to her, "You shall live a life scorned by other girls; you will be treated as a giddy and conceited hussy, or a poor half-mad wretch, or a wanton woman, etc.," and you will be exposed to every other kind of suffering.

    —Søren Kierkegaard

❀ Kierkegaard expresses extreme compassion for the social ostracism that Mary would have experienced in her rigidly religious environment upon learning, while engaged to Joseph, that she was pregnant with a child not fathered by Joseph. But Kierkegaard opens his comments with high praise for her, as though he were thinking of one of the Beatitudes (which he loved): "Blessed are you when men hate you, and when they exclude you, and revile you, and cast out your name as evil, on account of the son of man" (Luke 6:22).

At Peace in the Presence of God

Mary, our lady, spoke with her thought to our lord as often as she wished, and so his Godhead sometimes answered her. Therefore, she bore her suffering in a seemly manner. For this, Mary Magdalene was unprepared. When she did not see our lord with fleshly eyes then she was uncomforted, and her heart bore all the while great sorrow and discomfort. She burned greatly in simple love, without the high knowledge of heavenly things, until the hour when the apostles received the Holy Spirit. Then for the first time her soul was wounded with the Godhead. But our lady was very still, when our lord rose up from the dead so nobly. Her heart had in godly knowledge the deepest ground of all humans.

—Mechthild of Magdeburg

❖ The author of the mystical classic *The Flowing Light of the Godhead*, Mechthild of Magdeburg (c. 1212–1282), was, like Hadewijch (see page 133), a Beguine, a member of a sacred women's movement in medieval Europe. Beguines lived communally and followed the Christian life of prayer and service without taking religious vows. Her book is in essence a very beautiful and theologically refined expression of the soul's experiences during a prolonged and ardent spiritual journey. Mechthild influenced Meister Eckhart and may have been the "Matelda" mentioned by Dante in the *Divine Comedy*.

Sub Tuum

We place ourselves in your keeping, holy Mother of God. Hear the prayer of your children in their distress and protect us from all danger, O you who are so blessed.

—Anonymous

❖ Dated between the third and eighth centuries by various scholars, this lovely prayer is one of Christianity's earliest extant prayers.

Stabat Mater

At the cross, her station keeping,
Stood the mournful mother weeping,
Close to Jesus to the last:
Through her heart, his sorrow sharing,
All his bitter anguish bearing,
Now at length the sword had passed.
—Medieval hymn

�֍ The *Stabat Mater* has been set to music by Palestrina, Rossini, Dvořak, and many other composers and exists in dozens of versions. It belongs to the popular medieval genre of *Marienklagen*, in which Mary laments the anguished loss of her son.

And has Our Lady lost her place?
    Does her white star burn dim?
Nay, she has lowly veiled her face
    Because of Him....
She claims no crown from Christ apart,
    Who gave God life and limb,
She only claims a broken heart,
    Because of Him.
    —G. A. Studdert Kennedy

Love and Sorrow

I saw part of the compassion of our Lady, St. Mary, for Christ and she were so united in love that the greatness of her love was the cause of the greatness of her pain. For in this I saw a substance of natural love, which is developed by grace, which his creatures have for him, and this natural love was most perfectly and surpassingly revealed in his sweet mother. For as much as she loved him more than all others, her pain surpassed that of all others. For always, the higher, the stronger, the sweeter that love is, the more sorrow it is to the lover to see the body which he loved in pain. And so all his disciples and all his true lovers suffered more pain than they did at the death of their own bodies. For I am sure, by my own experience, that the least of them loved him so much more than they did themselves that it surpasses all that I can say.

—Julian of Norwich

❖ | Here Julian reflects on her "Showings," the series of visions she experienced during a near-fatal illness. Having seen at firsthand in the showing the extent of Christ's suffering on the day of his life, she becomes aware that one suffers with the suffering beloved.

What crime, what indignity
this harsh people has perpetrated
chains, whip, wounds,
nails, thorns, a cross' death
he acquired with no fault....

Hunger, death blow, every need,
you experience yet what it means
that you saw your Jesus dead
and Barabbas living on.
　　　—Godfrey of St. Victor

❖ These deeply moving lines by the Victorine monk Godfrey (d. c. 1194), in which he imagines Mary speaking at the foot of the cross, may be read as an accusation against the Roman men who executed Christ. It is virtually impossible, however, to imagine the sentiment coming from a mother in unspeakable grief.

A Sword Will Pierce Your Soul

You [Mary] will be exposed to every other possible kind of suffering, and at the end, a sword will pierce through your soul ... when you see that God himself will seem to have abandoned you.... These swords (Luke 2:35) are a parenthesis in the prophecy of Christ becoming a sign. They reveal the thoughts of many hearts. So they must not merely be taken to refer to the pain at the sight of the son's death [to the contrary]. As Christ cries, "my God, my God, why hast Thou forsaken me?" so the Virgin Mary had to suffer something that corresponded in a human way to his suffering.

—Søren Kierkegaard

To feel oneself forsaken by God is part of the complete emptying of the human element in the face of God.

—Søren Kierkegaard

❖ The two entries from Kierkegaard's journal and the passage from Philippians become clearer in the light of the notion of *kenosis*, or self-emptying: the state of complete letting go that Jesus underwent on the cross when he aligned himself totally with his understanding of God's will.

Kierkegaard is saying in the two entries from his journal that when Mary stood with her tortured and crucified son, facing his agony, powerless to alter the course of events, she must have shared Jesus' desolate sense of forsakenness and experienced her own self-emptying. But Kierkegaard adds that the *kenosis* undergone by the mother of God is not the same as that experienced by her divine son: Mary is emptied-out "in a human way."

(continued on next page)

His state was divine,
yet he did not cling
to his equality with God
but emptied himself
to assume the condition of a slave,
and became as men are;
and being as all men are,
he was humbler yet,
even to accepting death,
death on a cross.
      —Philippians 2:6–11

Kierkegaard, one of the great Christian thinkers of all time, grounds this belief in his reading of Simeon's prophecy, which took place when Mary and Joseph presented the infant Jesus in the temple. At that time, Simeon said to Mary that her child "is destined for the fall and rising of many in Israel, destined to be a sign that is rejected—and a sword will pierce your own soul, too" (Luke 2:33–35). Just as a Roman soldier drove his sword into Jesus' side to be certain he had died, a symbolic sword broke into her heart as she watched her beloved son die.

With Jesus in the Garden of Gethsemane

Mary left the place where she was staying to meet Jesus on the way. When they met, the prince of Eternity and the Queen, face to face, a sword of sorrow pierced the hearts of each of them, inflicting a pain of grief surpassing anything that either a human being or an angel could imagine. The sorrowful mother threw herself at the feet of the son, worshiping him as her God and Savior. The Lord, Divine majesty visible in his eyes, looked at her with a son's overflowing love, and said only this: "Mother, I will be with you in affliction; let us accomplish the will of God and the salvation of humankind." With her whole heart, the great Queen offered herself as a sacrifice, and requested his blessing. She then returned to her retreat where she received from the risen Lord a special consolation: she would know all that passed concerning her Divine Son.

    —Mary of Agreda
    (abridged)

❖ In this imaginative passage from *The Mystical City of God*, Blessed Mary of Agreda (Sister Mary of Jesus in religious life) probably intends to connote the Trinity when she uses the word "us" in line 10. Today, many seekers read the sentence as connecting Mary to the redeeming work of her son, a much debated idea. While some theologians have called Mary Co-Redemptrix (or Co-Redeemer) with Jesus, others assign her a secondary place in salvation history.

Star of this stormy sea,...
Turn your heart to the terrifying squall
In which I find myself,
alone,
without a map.
> —Petrarch

❖ The Italian poet, scholar, and humanist Petrarch, or Francesco Petrarca (1304–1374), paved the way toward the attitudes of the Renaissance.

Mary's Heart Will Triumph

During the last 150 years, Mary has been appearing all over the world, delivering short, simple messages of infinite love, wisdom, and urgency, trying to wake her children up to the enormity of the danger they are facing and to the remedies of prayer, mutual honor, and hard work in every dimension that alone can save the situation....

"My immaculate heart will triumph," Mary said to the children at Fatima, after being terrifyingly clear about the dangers ahead. Mary's heart—and the heart of her Son—will triumph, but only if we all turn to them now, with humility and confidence and complete lack of illusion about the potentially terminal danger we are in.

—Andrew Harvey

❖ At Banneux, Medjugorje, Fatima, and many other sites where people have been experiencing visions of Mary since c. 1850, the messages received by visionaries often center on peace and prayer.

These are the times of the great return. Yes, after the time
of the great suffering, there will be the time of the great
rebirth, and all will blossom again. Humanity will again be
a new garden of life and beauty.
  —Medjugorje visionary

⌘ A young visionary reported hearing Mary deliver this message in
Medjugorje, in the former Yugoslavia, in 1986.

Grieve not that Mary has gone;
the light that Jesus heavenward bore—
has come!
　　—Jalal-ud-Din Rumi

8

On Pilgrimage with Mary

God speaks:

You see this gentle loving word born in a stable while Mary was on a journey, to show you, a pilgrim, how you should be constantly reborn in the stable of self-knowledge. There, by grace, you will find me birthed within your soul.

—Catherine of Siena

⊕ The twenty-fourth of twenty-five children, Catherine of Siena was born in 1347 to a devout, well-to-do family in a beautiful home, which may still be visited today, near the center of Siena. She experienced spiritual visions from the age of six on, and at eighteen she retired to a tiny room in the basement of the home to devote herself to silent, solitary prayer. After three years of intense inner experience, she emerged transformed, a mystic of love and truth, a political activist committed to church reform and to teaching others the way of prayer. Here she emphasizes the necessity of self-knowledge on the mystical path. Like most mystics in most of the world's mystical traditions, she teaches that the way to the truest knowledge of God is through the self.

If Mary protects me
Her divine son
will receive me
into the company of the saints
who walk with him in paradise.

Like a lost sheep
whose shepherd is searching for it,
Seek me, Mother of mercy.
Bring me safely home....
    —Raissa Maritain

❧ Born to a Jewish family in Russia in 1883, Raissa and her family
migrated to France in 1893. At the Sorbonne, she met her future husband, the philosopher Jacques Maritain, and with him took a vow to
commit suicide if they could not find a way to see meaning in life's
tragedies. Under the influence of the Catholic writer Leon Bloy, they
were baptized Catholics in 1906, and Raissa, a natural mystic,
embraced the contemplative life. *Raissa's Journal* is a classic in mystical literature.

Midday. I see the open church.
It draws me within.
I did not come, Mother of Jesus Christ,
to pray.
I have nothing to offer you.
Nor to ask of you.
I only come, O my Mother,
To gaze at you,
To see you, to cry simply out of joy.
Because I know that I am your child,
And that you are there.

—Paul Claudel

This poem of the twentieth-century French writer Paul Claudel describes a decisive moment in his faith life when he was recovering an awareness of the presence of God and of Mary's role as mediator between God and humankind.

The Return of Mary

One of the intriguing aspects of the latest rise of Mary is this: the emotional need for her is so irresistible to a troubled world that people without an obvious link to the Virgin are being drawn to her. It's not news that Muslims revere Mary as a pure and holy saint— ... she's mentioned thirty-four times in the Koran, which upholds her virginal conception of Jesus—but to see large numbers of Muslims making pilgrimages to Christian Marian shrines is a remarkable thing. Inter-denominational Marian prayer groups are springing up throughout the world.

—*Life* magazine, December, 1996

Christians and Muslims alike can see in Mary an affirmation that there is no limit to the holiness, or proximity to God, that any human, whether male of female, can attain.

—The *Economist*, December 20, 2003

�֍ Mary's presence in human awareness has waxed and waned throughout Christian history. Her most recent reappearance—in the 1980s and 1990s—is the most widespread of all time among both churched and unchurched people and is growing continually.

A Priest's Prayer of Self-Dedication to Mary

Most Holy Virgin Mary, perfect disciple of Jesus, I come to dedicate my life and my priestly ministry to your Immaculate Heart. I desire to abandon myself to the will of Jesus, your son, and walk in faith with you, my Mother. To you I consecrate my life in the priesthood. I give you every gift I possess of nature and of grace, my body and my soul, all that I own and everything I do. Pray for me that the Holy Spirit may visit me with his many gifts. Pray for me, that by faith I may know the power of Christ and by love make him present in the world. Amen.

—Source unknown

�֍ Many priests begin their day by reciting this beautiful prayer.

On Pilgrimage with Mary

Go with the mother and child as they flee into Egypt.
Accompany them. Keep searching with the worried mother
looking for her son until you find him. Imagine how it
  would feel
to look with devotion at such a great woman, such a young
  girl,
in a foreign country with a gentle little boy? Imagine
  hearing
the loving reprimand of the mother of God: "Son, why have
  you done this to us?" as if she were saying: My beloved
  son, how could you give so much anxiety to your mother,
  whom you love,
and who loves you so much?

        —Bonaventure

�֍ Bonaventure is alluding here to two Christian Scriptures stories: the flight into Egypt to escape Herod's persecution (Matthew 2:13–23), and Mary's loss of her young son during the three days when he remained at the temple in Jerusalem without telling his parents where he was (Luke 2:41–52).

Why do we have to search for Mary? Aren't we constantly running into her as it is? Not just in churches and on Christmas cards, but in museums, and even in some backyards—to say nothing of her shrines at Lourdes, Guadalupe, Fatima, and now Medjugorje? For the 1995 Christmas season, the U. S. Postal service issued seven hundred million stamps bearing the image of the Madonna and Child created by the fourteenth-century Florentine painter Giotto di Bondone. An angel had been slated to replace Mary, but popular demand brought back her image. Even the last desperate pass of a losing football team is known as a "Hail Mary" play.

—Sally Cunneen

Salve Regina

Hail Holy Queen
Mother of Mercy,
our life,
our sweetness,
and our hope.
To you do we cry,
poor banished children of Eve,
to you do we send up our sighs,
mourning and weeping
in this valley of tears.
Turn then, most gracious advocate,
your eyes of mercy toward us;
and after this our exile,
show to us the blessed fruit
of your womb, Jesus.
O clement, O loving, O sweet virgin Mary.
   —Attributed to Adhemar, Bishop of le Puy

❧ One can imagine the Crusaders chanting this melancholy prayer while marching to battle and possibly death. It was probably composed in the eleventh century when physical pain, hunger, and cruelty ended most lives early. Adhemar of Monteil, Bishop of Le Puy, the unifying force and leader of the First Crusade, was not only a forceful churchman but also a highly successful warrior. He died of the plague while on crusade.

Happily, monks at Mount St. Bernard's Abbey created a warmer, more positive, and more joyful version of his *Salve Regina*, which brings out Mary's motherliness. It is the next selection.

A New *Salve Regina*

We greet you, holy Queen,
our life, our joy and our hope,
Mother full of mercy, we cry to you in trust.
Exiled children of fallen Eve,
see our sighs and tears,
see our world of sadness.
Mother, plead for us.
Turn then towards us those eyes that plead our cause,
and when our life on earth is done,
show us then your Son,
blessed fruit of your virgin womb,
Jesus Christ our God.
O Mary, full of kindness,
O Mary, full of love,
O joyful Mary, full of peace and grace.

    —Mount St. Bernard's Abbey

From *The Spiritual Canticle*

The discreet lover does not care to ask for what she lacks and desires, but only indicates this need that the Beloved may do what He pleases. When the Blessed Virgin spoke to her beloved son at the wedding feast in Cana in Galilee, she did not ask directly for the wine, but merely remarked: *They have no wine* (John 2:3). And the sisters of Lazarus did not send to ask our Lord to cure their brother, but to tell him that Lazarus whom he loved was sick (John 11:3). There are three reasons for this: first, the Lord knows what is suitable for us better than we do; second, the Beloved has more compassion when He beholds the need and resignation of a soul that loves Him; third, the soul is better safeguarded against self-love and possessiveness by indicating its lack, rather than asking for what in its opinion is wanting. The soul, now, does likewise by just indicating her three needs. Her words are similar to saying: Tell my beloved, since I sicken and He alone is my health, to give me health; and since I suffer and He alone is my

---

�֍ The "Mystical Doctor," John of the Cross (1542–1591), was one of the world's most discerning, sensitive, profound, and loving contemplatives and, like his grand friend, Teresa of Ávila, a spiritual treasure for all who knew him. The selection above comes from the deepest levels of mystical understanding and wisdom and can be grasped only through faith and love. He is commenting on the second stanza of his magnificent mystical poem, *The Spiritual Canticle*, which refers to the mystical journey of the soul through three stages of letting go, illumination, and oneness with God. The stanza refers to the ascent of the pilgrim seeking God in the summits of love:

(continued on next page)

joy, to give me joy; and, since I die and He alone is my life, to give me life.

—John of the Cross
Translated by Kieran Kavanaugh, O.C.D.,
and Otilio Rodriguez, O.C.D.

Shepherds, you that go
Up through the sheepfolds to the hill,
If by any chance you see
Him I love most,
Tell him that I sicken, suffer, and die.

The reader needs to think symbolically about the shepherd's journey to penetrate the many layers of meaning in John's commentary above. His reference to Mary comes partly from passionate devotion to her, whom he credits for all the graces of his life. (Once, preaching at mass, he noticed a picture of Mary and exclaimed: "How happy I would be to live alone in a desert with that image!")

Honoring Mary with a Special Love

In celebrating the annual cycle of the mysteries of Christ, Holy Church honors the Blessed Mary, Mother of God, with a special love. She is inseparably with her Son's saving work. In her, the church admires and exalts the most excellent fruit of redemption, and joyfully contemplates, as in a faultless image, that which it itself desires and hopes to be.

—From *The Constitution on the Sacred Liturgy,*
Second Vatican Council

The Blessing of St. Clare

May the Lord bless and keep you. May He show his face to you and be merciful to you. May he turn his countenance to you and give you peace.

I, Clare, a servant of Christ, a small plant of our holy Father Francis, a sister and mother of you and the other Poor Sisters, although unworthy, ask our Lord Jesus Christ through his mercy and through the intercession of His Most Holy Mother Mary, of blessed Michael Archangel and of all the holy angels of God, and of all His men and women saints, that the heavenly Father give you and confirm for you this most holy blessing in heaven and on earth. On earth, may He increase His grace and virtues among the men and women servants of His church militant. In heaven, may He exalt and glorify you in His church triumphant among all His men and women saints.

I bless you in my life and after my death as much as I can and more than I can with all the blessings with which the Father of mercies has and will have blessed His sons and daughters in heaven and on earth.

✤ The two mystical saints of Assisi, Francis (c. 1182–1226) and Clare (c. 1194–1253), represent the West's first protest against obscene wealth and materialism. While many men and women before them had renounced inheritances and titles to embrace a life of prayer and fasting, Francis and Clare took a giant step forward by bringing radical, communal poverty to the forefront of religious life. Today Clare's cloak may be seen, well patched from decades of use, hanging in the basilica named for her in Assisi. Clare was also the author of the first rule for governing a religious community ever written by a woman. She revered Mary in her role as intercessor with God.

Always be lovers of God and your souls and the souls of your Sisters, and always be eager to observe what you have promised the Lord.

May the Lord be with you always and, wherever you are, may you be with Him always. Amen.

—Attributed to Clare of Assisi

The Happy Fall

As Eve was seduced by the word of [a fallen] angel to avoid God after she had disobeyed his word, so Mary, by the word of an angel, had the glad tiding delivered to her that she might give birth to God obeying his word. Whereas Eve had disobeyed God, yet the latter chose to obey God in order that the Virgin Mary might be the advocate of the

---

�֎ Early Christian thinkers were as captivated as people have been ever since by the story of the Garden of Eden (Genesis 3:1–24). Why did the serpent slither into Paradise—from where no one knows—and totally disrupt the enchanting natural beauty, the ecological health and fruitfulness, the ideally happy relationship between mankind and womankind that God had created there? Church fathers and mothers, in all parts of the expanding Christian world, painstakingly sought explanations to these troubling questions in the scriptures.

Among them were Irenaeus (c. 120/140–c. 200/203) as bishop of Lyons in today's France, Justin Martyr (c. 100–c. 165) and Tertullian (c. 155/160–c. 230) in today's Near East, and Origen (c. 185–c. 254) in Carthage in North Africa, among others, who took up the theme of Mary as the second Eve, so called because she undoes the damage caused by Eve. Thus, the apparently tragic fall of humankind will be called the happy fall, to indicate that the shadow of original sin has a very bright side because it leads to the world-transforming birth of the Christ, as well as Mary's timeless power and intercession in human life.

Presumably, the Church fathers had in mind Paul's remarks such as I Corinthians 15:22 (notice that here Paul places the responsibility for original sin on the first man, rather than the first woman):

As in Adam all die, so in Christ shall all be made alive.

(continued on next page)

virgin Eve…. The guile of the serpent was overcome by the simplicity of the dove, and we were set free from those chains by which we had been bound to death.

—Irenaeus

Or Romans 5:12:

[S]in entered the world through one man, and through sin death, and thus death has spread through the whole human race because everyone has sinned….

Or Romans 5:15b:

… it is certain that through one man's fall so many died….

Just as Christ is the new Adam, so is Mary the new Eve.

Prayer for Peace

Sancta Maria, ora pro nobis!
Pray, O Mother, for all of us.
Pray for humanity that suffers poverty and injustice,
violence and hatred, terror and war.
Help us to contemplate with the holy rosary
the mysteries of him who "is our peace."
So that we will feel involved
in a specific effort of service to peace.

Look with special attention
upon the land in which you gave birth to Jesus,
a land that you loved together
and that is still so tried today.

Pray for us, Mother of Hope!
"Give us days of peace, watch over our way.
Let us see your Son
full of joy in heaven!" Amen.
        —Attributed to Pope John Paul II

⚜ On the feast of the Immaculate Conception on December 8, 2002,
in Rome, Pope John Paul II included this prayer in a sermon when he
was speaking about Mary.

I God
am in your midst.

Whoever knows me
can never fall.

    Not
        in the heights,
            nor in the depths,
                nor in the breadths.

For I am Love

which the vast expanses of evil
can never still.
        —Hildegard of Bingen

✽ The context of this beautiful poem relates to God's self-disclosure in Mary's son.

Before the sunrise
We the children of Africa,
We praise you, Mary, joyfully …
You are black but beautiful …
We love you more than
the sounds of drumming after dusk.
　　　—Anonymous

⸎ This song, which is accompanied by a dance, is part of a contemporary African Catholic liturgy. Line 4, "you are black but beautiful," comes from the Hebrew Scriptures: Song of Songs 1:5.

Del Verbo Divino

The Virgin, weighed
with the word of God,
Comes down the road:
If only you'll shelter her.

—John of the Cross
Translated by Kieran Kavanaugh, O.C.D.,
and Otilito Rodriguez, O.C.D.

❖ *Del Verbo Divino* is Latin for "On the Word of God."

Christmas Season Commemoration of Mary

The Christmas season is a prolonged commemoration of the divine, virginal, and salvific Motherhood of her whose "inviolate virginity brought the Savior into the world." In fact, on the solemnity of the Birth of Christ the church adores the Savior and venerates his glorious Mother. On the Epiphany, when she celebrates the universal call to salvation, the Church contemplates the Blessed Virgin, the true seat of Wisdom and true Mother of the King, who presents to the Wise Men for their adoration the Redeemer of all peoples. On the feast of the Holy Family of Jesus … the church meditates with profound reverence upon the holy life led in the home at Nazareth by Jesus, the Son of God and the Son of Man, Mary his Mother, and Joseph, the just man (cf. Matthew 1:19).

—Pope Paul VI

⁂ By emphasizing the vastness of Mary's importance on three separate occasions during the Christmas season, Pope Paul was calling for renewed veneration of her in the era of lapsed devotion that followed the Second Vatican Council in the 1960s. The Advent season, too, is a special time to commemorate Mary as the ideal model of waiting for God.

9
In Praise of Mary

I see you in a thousand paintings
Mary, so tenderly depicted
Yet none of them can begin to show you
As my soul sees you.

I only know that the world's chaos
Has suddenly vanished like a dream,
And a heaven of ineffable sweetness
Has opened forever in my soul.
    —Novalis

�֎ Novalis was the pen name of the early German Romantic poet
Friedrich von Hardenberg (1772–1801). His works and theories influenced most later Romantic writers in Germany, France, and England.

Ave Maria! 'tis the hour of prayer!
    Ave Maria! 'tis the hour of love!
Ave Maria! May our spirits dare
    Look up to thine and to thy Son's above!
Ave Maria!

—Lord Byron

These famous lines from Lord Byron's *Don Juan*, Canto III, although penned by a relative nonbeliever, convey the holiness of the love experienced in deep prayer. George Gordon, Lord Byron (1788–1824), was a celebrated poet and satirist in England, whose attitude of ironic despair and aspirations for personal liberty captured the imagination of Europe and made him the universal symbol of the Romantic period.

Mary, Star of the Sea

If the storms of temptation arise, if you crash against the rocks of tribulation, look to the star, call upon Mary. If you are tossed about on the waves of pride, of ambition, of slander, of hostility, look to the star, call upon Mary.... If you begin to be swallowed up by the abyss of depression and despair, think of Mary! In dangers, in anxiety, in doubt, think of Mary, call upon Mary.... When you are terrified by judgment or in despair, think of Mary for if she holds you, you will never fail. If she protects you, you need not fear.

—Bernard of Clairvaux

Blessed Are You, My Lady Virgin Mary

Blessed are you, my Lady Virgin Mary, most holy Mother of God, whose noblest creature you are, and who was never so loved as by you.

Blessed are you, my Lady Virgin Mary, who felt the body of Christ, created from your own blessed body, grow and move in your womb till the time of his glorious nativity; whom you before all others touched with your sacred hands, wrapped in swaddling cloths, and according to the prophecy, laid in a manger to nurture him.

Blessed are you, my Lady Virgin Mary, who knew in advance that your son would be arrested and afterwards, so sadly, saw him with your own eyes bound and scourged, crowned with thorns and fastened naked to the cross.

Blessed are you, O Mother of God, glorious Lady Virgin Mary, and exult, for you were permitted to see your body revived after death, assumed with your soul into heaven escorted by angels, where you see your son in jubilation,

�֎ Born to a noble family in Finsta, Sweden, Birgitta (1303–1373) at her parents' insistence married Prince Ulf of Nericia and gave birth to eight children, one of whom became Catherine of Sweden. Birgitta joined the Third Order Franciscans to use her wealth and energy in the world according to the ideals of Francis and Clare. She had a hospital built, founded a monastery, and, when she was widowed, engaged herself dramatically in politics. Brigitta wrote an influential book, *Revelations*. Journeying to the Holy Land, she experienced visions that have often

(continued on next page)

divinity with humanity, justly judge and reward good works.

Blessed and venerated are you, O my Lady Virgin Mary, that every faithful creature praises God for you, as you are God's most worthy creature, swift advocate obtaining forgiveness for souls.

—Birgitta of Sweden

been painted by prominent artists, such as Grunewald (the *Crucifixion*), and are widely reflected in music and literature as well as art. Today, the feudal language of her era somewhat obfuscates her love of Mary and her identification with her as a mother, but these deep feelings and beliefs surface in the maternal imagery in her work—which is typical of many women mystics, married or professed.

The all-golden vessel,
the most delectable sweetener of our souls,
she who bears the manna which is Christ,
land uncultivated,
field unploughed,
vine streaming with fecundity,
vessel most delightful,
spring that gushes forth,
the treasure of innocence
and ornament of modesty
    —Byzantine sermon

❖ The extravagant language in this eighth-century Eastern sermon in praise of Mary is thought to have originated in Jewish and Christian Wisdom literature, which addressed phrases of heart-stopping beauty to the personified figure of Wisdom. Many of the florid words associated with Lady Wisdom, who is *Hochma* in the Hebrew Scripture and *Sophia* (Greek for "wisdom") in the Christian Scripture, came to be applied to Jesus, while they even more became connected to Mary.

Antiphon

Holy Virgin Mary,
among women
there is no one like you born into the world:
you are the daughter
and the servant of the most high and supreme King
and Father of heaven,
you are the mother of our most holy Lord Jesus Christ,
you are the spouse of the Holy Spirit.
Pray for us
with Saint Michael the Archangel
and all the powers of the heavens
and all the saints
to your most holy beloved Son, the Lord and Master.
Glory be the Father
and to the Son
and to the Holy Spirit
as it was in the beginning
is now
and ever shall be.
Amen.
—Francis of Assisi

✤ Written by one of the West's most beloved saints, Francis of Assisi (c. 1182–1226), this antiphon belongs to his liturgy for the last three days of Holy Week—Holy Thursday, Good Friday, and Holy Saturday— as well as weekdays throughout the year. In his book *The Second Life of Saint Francis*, Thomas Celano writes that Francis' love for Mary was "inexpressible."

[T]he angelic love who had descended
earlier now spread his wings before her,
singing, *"Ave Maria, gratia plena."*
　　　—Dante Alighieri

❖ The selection comes from *The Divine Comedy*, *Paradiso* 32, 94–96.
Ave Maria, gratia plena is Latin for "Hail Mary, full of grace."

May is Mary's Month

May is Mary's month, and I
Muse at that and wonder why:
     Her feasts follow reason,
     Dated due to season—

Candlemas, Lady Day;
But the Lady Month, May,
     Why fasten that upon her?
     With a feasting in her honour?...

Ask of her, the mighty mother:
Her reply puts this other
     Question: What is spring?—
     Growth in every thing—

Flesh and fleece, fur and feather,
Grass and greenworld altogether;
     Star-eyed strawberry-breasted
     Throstle above her nested

Cluster of bugle blue eggs thin
Forms and warms the life within;
     And bird and blossom swell
     In sod or sheath or shell.

All things rising, all things sizing
Mary sees, sympathizing
     With that world of good,
     Nature's motherhood.
          —Gerard Manley Hopkins

Virgo Prudentissima

When the most wise Virgin,
who birthed Joy in the world,
went above all the spheres and
left the stars beneath her shining feet
in gleaming radiant light,
she was surrounded by the nine-fold ranks
hand received by the nine hierarchies.
She, the friend of suppliants,
stood before the face of the supreme God.

You who inhabit eternally
the dazzling lights of heaven—
you archangels,
you leaders of the spirits and angels,
you thrones of princes,
holy armies and powers,
you dominions of heaven,

⚘ "Ranks" refers to the nine orders (or choirs) of angels arranged as
the Bible describes them, in nine concentric circles. "Hierarchies"
alludes to Pseudo-Dionysius' Neoplatonic positioning of the angelic
orders vertically, as though on nine rising steps of a ladder. The "low-
est" angels, those closest to humankind, include the Angels and
Archangels, who appear in both the Hebrew Scriptures and the Christian Scriptures. The "highest," those closest to God, the Seraphim and
Cherubim, are found only in the Hebrew Scriptures (with one Christian Scriptures exception, Hebrews 9:5, which is derived from the
Hebrew Scriptures). Between the two extremes are five orders found
only in the Christian Scriptures: Virtues, Powers, Principalities, Domi-
nations, and Thrones.

(continued on next page)

fiery cherubim and seraphim,
created from the Word—
say whether such a feeling of joy
has ever overwhelmed you
as when you saw the assembly of
the Mother of the Everlasting Almighty!

O Queen, omnipotent in heaven
and on land and on sea,
O glorious tender Queen,
pray for us now and always,
and raise us into your glory!
        —Anonymous

Ark, fortress, tower, house, garden, mirror, fountain;
The sea, a star, the moon, the rose of dawn, a mountain;
She is another world, so can be all these things freely.

　　　—Angelus Silesius
　　　　Translated by Andrew Harvey

❖　Angelus Silesius was the pen name of Johannes Scheffler (1624–1677), a Polish mystic, Catholic polemicist, and poet, who wrote primarily religious songs.

Hail Mary
full of grace,
the Lord
is with you.
Blessed
are you
among women
and blessed
is the fruit
of your womb,
Jesus.
Holy Mary
Mother of God
pray for us
now
and at the hour of our death.
    Amen
        —Traditional

❖ This universal prayer took form gradually from the seventh century
on, but it was not widely used until the eleventh and twelfth centuries.
Its words come from the angel Gabriel and from Mary's cousin Elizabeth, in the first chapter of the gospel of Luke. The word "hail" is often
translated today as "rejoice."

Angelic Song of Praise

I am angelic love who wheel around
that high gladness inspired by the womb
that was the dwelling place of our Desire;
so shall I circle, Lady of Heaven, until
you, following your Son, have made that sphere
supreme, still more divine by entering it.
   —Dante Alighieri

❊ Here the holy "brightnesses" in Paradise, the angels, and the church triumphant sing to Mary, "the greatest flame" (*The Divine Comedy, Paradiso* 23, 103–108).

O Lord, we praise and magnify your Name
For the Most Holy Virgin Mother of God,
Who is the highest of your saints,
The most glorious of all your creatures,
The most perfect of all your works,
The nearest to you, in the throne of God,
Whom you were pleased to make
Daughter of the Eternal Father,
Mother of the Eternal Son,
Spouse of the Eternal Spirit,
Tabernacle of the most glorious Trinity.
Mother of Jesus,
Mother of the Messiah,
Mother of the Desire of Nations,
Mother of the Prince of Peace,
Mother of the King of Heaven,
Mother of our Creator,
Mother and Virgin,
Mirror of humility and obedience,
Mirror of wisdom and devotion,
Mother of modesty and chastity,
Mirror of sweetness and resignation,
Mirror of sanctity,
Mirror of all virtues.
        —Thomas Traherne

❖ This rapturous seventeenth-century litany reveals widespread accep-
tance of Mary as the Divine Mother, the feminine face of God. The
English poet Thomas Traherne lived from 1637 to 1674.

O how wondrous is Your love!
You gazed on your fairest daughter
As an eagle focuses its eye upon the sun;
You, the eternal Father, saw
her radiance,
and the Word became flesh in her.
            —Hildegard of Bingen

✤ In the Middle Ages, an eagle symbolized the contemplative's inner
eye focusing on God in deep, silent prayer. What is remarkable here is
Hildegard's placement of Mary rather than God as the object of contemplation.

The Happy Fall

Had not the apple taken been,
    The apple taken been.
Had never our Lady
    Been heaven's queen.
Blessed be the time
    That apple taken was!
Because of that we sing
      "Deo gratias!"
        —Anonymous fifteenth-century poem

❖ The theme of the "happy fall," the *felix culpa,* appears as early as
the fourth century in the writings of Ambrose (339–397), the German
lawyer who was consecrated bishop of Milan the same week he was
baptized. For him, as for the anonymous poet here, the Fall became a
source of joy as it led to the incarnation, through Mary's motherhood
of the Savior.

Truly, O noble Virgin, you are great and above all greatness. Who indeed can compare with your greatness, O dwelling place of the word of God? With whom shall I compare you among all creatures? You are evidently greater than all of them. O Ark of the covenant surrounded totally and purely on all sides with gold! You are the Ark containing all gold, the receptacle of the true manna, that is human, and in which the Divine resides. Shall I not compare you with the fecund earth and its fruits?... Indeed, you bear within yourself the feet and head and entire body of a god. Even if I speak of the highest heaven it will not compare to you; for it is written, "Heaven is my throne" (Is. 66:1) for you are the dwelling place of God. Should I speak of the angels and the archangels, you are greater than they; for the angels and archangels serve with wonder the one who is contained within you, nor do they dare to speak in his presence, while you speak freely with him. If I speak of the great Cherubim, you excel even them. If I speak of the Seraphim, you are greater still; they indeed cover their face with their wings not having perfect glory, while you not only contemplate the face, but kiss the sacred mouth and nourish it with your breasts.

—Athanasius

❖ A great Mariologist and convert to Christianity from Egypt, Athanasius (295–373) was one of the first people to call Mary *Theotokos*, or Mother of God. He wrote this exuberant passage not only in praise of Mary but to affirm his belief in the divinity of Christ in opposition to a priest named Arius, who had aroused a raging controversy about the true nature of Christ by denying his divinity. In 325, the church convened a council at Nicaea that sided with Athanasius and his followers against Arius' movement with the publication of the Nicene Creed, naming Jesus as "true God of true God."

Ave Regina

Ave Regina,
holy, loving,
most noble queen.
Ave Maris Stella.
Star of the Sea,
Moon where God took hiding.
But for the Virgin Mary
The world had been lost.

—Anonymous fourteenth-century penitential song

✤ *Ave Regina* is Latin for "Hail, queen," and *Ave Maris Stella* means "Hail, Star of the Sea."

Mary,
If I were Queen of Heaven,
and you were Théresè,
I would pray to be Théresè
for you to be Queen of Heaven.
—Théresè of Lisieux

Popularly known as the Little Flower, Théresè of the Child Jesus (1873–1897) came from a family with a strong devotion to Mary that named its eight sons and daughters for her. All four daughters entered the Carmelite convent at Lisieux, Théresè receiving special permission to enter early at the age of only fifteen. She concealed a secret ambition to be a priest. Original, courageous, impassioned for God, and very wise for her years, she rejected the prevalent spirituality of rigid conformity in favor of her own path, her "little way" of simplicity, love, and a famous promise to "spend my Heaven doing good on earth." At the moment of death after extreme and prolonged suffering from tuberculosis, Théresè's face suddenly radiated light. She raised her head, looked up, and exclaimed with great joy: "Oh, I love him. My God, I love you."

And there I saw a loveliness that when
it smiled at the angelic songs and games
made glad the eyes of all the other saints.
And even if my speech were rich as my
imagination is, I should not try
to tell the very least of her delights.
  —Dante Alighieri

❖ These beautiful lines come from *The Divine Comedy, Paradiso* 31, 133–38.

From the Akathistos Hymn

Rejoice, ray of the spiritual Sun!
Rejoice, flash of unfading splendor!

Rejoice, lightning that lights up our souls!
Rejoice, thunder that stuns our enemies!
Rejoice, for you caused the refulgent light to dawn!
Rejoice, for you caused the river of many streams to gush
  forth!
Rejoice, living image of the font!
Rejoice, remover of the stain of sin!
Rejoice, laver that washes the conscience clean!
Rejoice, bowl for mixing the wine of joy!
Rejoice, aroma of the fragrance of Christ!
Rejoice, life of mystical festivity!
Rejoice, unwedded bride!

> —Romanos Melodos
> Version by Andrew Harvey

✤ The author of this magnificent sixth-century prayer of praise, the Syrian poet Romanos Melodus, embraces the full mystical glory of Mary as *Theotokos*, the Mother of God. By mingling cosmic symbols such as "lightning" and "stars" with earthly images, such as "key," "wall," and "sheltering branches," he describes Mary as the one person other than her son in whom the opposites coexist: The human and the holy, virginity and motherhood, heaven and earth unite in her. She is the "ladder in the firmament" connecting earth to heaven so that God can descend to humankind, and men and women can ascend to God.* Some scholars think that Mary's role as a bridge is implicit in the story of Jacob's ladder in the Hebrew Scriptures (see Genesis 28:12).

*Not all of these images appear in the version of the hymn quoted here.

Our Lord showed this to me to make us glad and merry.... And with the same joyful appearance he looked down on his right, and brought to my mind where our Lady stood at the time of his Passion, and he said, "Do you wish to see her?" And these sweet words were as if he had said, "I know well that you wish to see my blessed mother, for after myself, she is the greatest joy that I could show you, and the greatest delight and honour to me, and she is what all my blessed creatures most desire to see." And because of the wonderful, exalted, and singular love that he has for this sweet maiden, his blessed mother, our Lady St. Mary, he reveals her bliss and joy through the sense of these sweet words, as if he said, "Do you wish to see how I love her, so that you could rejoice with me in the love which I have in her and she has in me?"

And for greater understanding of these sweet words ... he said, "Do you wish to see in her how you are loved? It is for love of you that I have made her so exalted, so noble, so honourable; and this delights me. And I wish it to

---

�֎ Julian of Norwich (1343–1416) was an anchoress (secluded nun) attached to the church of Saint Julian at Conisford in Norwich, England. On May 8, 1373, during an apparent near-death experience, she received a series of visions that she described and pondered in her "book of revelations," *Showings*, which appears in two versions: an early "Short Text" and a later "Long Text."

Showings lays open Julian's joyful and loving nature, her keen theological insight, and her trust in herself and her own wisdom over the authorities'. Among her most radical insights was her belief that "As truly as God is our Father, so truly is God our Mother."

(continued on next page)

delight you." For next to him she is the most blissful to be seen. But in this matter, I was not taught to long to see her bodily presence while I am here, but the virtues of her blessed soul, her truth, her wisdom, her love, through which I am taught to know myself and reverently stand in awe before God.

—Julian of Norwich

Afterword: ☐
Spiritual Practices Dedicated to Mary

One day you finally knew
what you had to do, and began.

MARY OLIVER

Spiritual practice accomplishes what nothing else in life can: the miracle of awakening to a new vision of yourself and imagining a new way of being in the world. From this broader and happier perspective, you may be surprised to find how wide your heart can open, how tenderly you can express yourself, and how deeply caring you can be when responding to the needs and hurts of others. But this is precisely what happens when you have a daily spiritual practice.

Few devotional exercises are more powerful than those dedicated to Mary, intercessor and helper, whose heart is always open to human prayers and who responds with gifts of comfort, strength, protection, and peace. Here is a selection of spiritual practices you may wish to try:

Begin any kind of activity with a prayer to Mary: a meal, a task at work, an exam, an athletic event, a doctor's appointment, a difficult meeting, and each time you leave the house or return. There are virtually unlimited occasions to grace with a brief prayer.

Carry a rosary with you and pray it with devotion whenever you can—for instance, when waiting in line or for an appointment, or to calm stress.

Find a prayer partner with whom you can pray the rosary, "Hail Mary," and improvised prayers to Mary, and with whom you can share spiritual ideas and feelings.

Set aside time to listen to songs, chants, or classical compositions written about Mary. Try chanting yourself.

Every morning, make several genuflections or bows to her. Some people make a hundred; for others, one is sufficient.

Create your own Mary mantra, a Mary prayer composed of only a few words, such as "Mary, Mother of us all, give me strength" (or wisdom, patience, generosity—whatever spiritual gift you need in the moment). Also, "Mary be with my friend [add name]." Or simply "I love you" or "Thank you." The possibilities are endless. Silently recite your Mary mantra to calm anxiety, contain anger, alleviate stress, help others, and so on.

At bedtime, look back on the blessings received that day, and thank Mary for them.

Create a Mary altar in your home. Give your imagination free rein. You may wish to place a picture or statue of her on a special table with favorite objects such as the Bible, a candle, flowers, incense, a stone, or a shell. If you wish, create your own image of Mary: Try painting, drawing, sculpting, making a collage, sewing, or any other medium you enjoy.

Find ways to give back to the community—for example, by giving money and goods to the poor, by tithing, by committing yourself to a form of service suitable to your own gifts and desires—and do it for Mary.

Honor Mary as the Mother of God by meditating on her words, virtues, and actions; and by contemplating what is great about her.

Perform acts of love for her without expectations of praise or a reward.

Before you sit down to pray or meditate (ideally at the same time and place each day), invoke Mary's presence as you would welcome a person you love.

At the close of your prayer or meditation session, offer yourself to her; consecrate your life to her.

Suggested Readings and Resources ☐

Selected Bibliography

Anselm of Canterbury. *The Prayers and Meditations of St. Anselm.* Translated by Benedicta Ward. Baltimore: Penguin Books, 1973.

Armstrong, Regis J., O.F.M., and Ignatius C. Brady, O.F.M., editors. *Francis and Clare: The Complete Works.* The Classics of Western Spirituality Series. New York: Paulist Press, 1982.

Ashe, Geoffery, *The Virgin.* London: Routledge and Kegan Paul, 1976.

Baring, Anne, and Jules Cashford. *The Myth of the Goddess: The Evolution of an Image.* London: Arkana Penguin Books, 1993.

Bernard of Clairvaux, Saint. *A la louange de la vierge Mere.* Traduction par Marie-Imelda Huille et Joel Regnard. Paris: Editions du Cerf, 1993.

————. *On Loving God.* Commentary by Emero S. Steigman. Kalamazoo, MI: Cistercian Publications, 1995.

————. *Sermons sur la Cantique.* Texte latin de J Leclercq, H. Rochais, et Ch. H. Talbot. Traduction par Paul Verdeyen at Raffaele Fassetta. Paris: Editions du Cerf, 1996.

Boff, Leonardo. *The Maternal Face of God: The Feminine and Its Religious Expressions.* San Francisco: Harper & Row, 1987.

Brown, Raymond E., et al., *Mary in the New Testament: A Collaborative Assessment by Protestant and Roman Catholic Scholars.* Philadelphia: Fortress Press, 1978.

Bruck, Anton Ph. *Hildegard von Bingen 1179–1979, Festschrift zum 800. Todestag der Heiligen.* Mainz: Selbstverlag der Gesellschaft fur Mittelrheinische Kirchengeschichte, 1979.

Campos, S. Alvarez. *Corpus marianum patristicum,* 3 vols. Burgos: Aldecoa, 1970–74.

Cappanari, Stephen C., and Leonard W. Moss. "Quest of the Black Virgin: She is black because she is black." In *Mother Worship: Themes and Variations*. Edited by James J. Preston. Chapel Hill: University of North Carolina Press, 1982.

Catherine of Siena. *The Dialogue*. Translated by Suzanne Noffke, O.P. The Classics of Western Spirituality Series. New York: Paulist Press, 1980.

Congar, Yves. "Marie et l'eglise dans la pensee patristique," RSPT 38 (1954).

Cunneen, Sally. *In Search of Mary: The Woman and the Symbol*. New York: Ballantine Books, 1996.

Doheney, Wm. J., and Joseph Kelly, compilers. *Papal Documents on Mary*. Milwaukee: Brunce Publishing, 1954.

Ehrman, Bart D. *Lost Christianities: The Battles for Scripture and the Faiths We Never Knew*. New York: Oxford University Press, 2003.

Eliot, Ethel Cook. "Our Lady of Guadalupe in Mexico." In *A Woman Clothed with the Sun*, edited by John J. Delaney, 39–60. Garden City, NY: Doubleday, 1990.

Epiphanius. *The Panarion of St. Epiphanius, Bishop of Salamis: Selected Passages*. Translated and edited by Philip R. Amidon, S. J. New York: Liberal Arts Press, 1957.

Eusebius. *Ecclesiastical History*. Baltimore: Penguin Books, 1965.

Fiorenza, Elizabeth Schussler. *Jesus: Miriam's Child, Sophia's Prophet*. New York: Continuum, 1994.

Flinders, Carol Lee. *Enduring Grace: Living Portraits of Seven Women Mystics*. San Francisco: HarperSanFrancisco, 1993.

Flusser, David, Jaroslav Pelikan, and Justin Lang. *Mary: Images of the Mother of Jesus in Jewish and Christian Perspectives*. Philadelphia: Fortress Press, 1986.

Foskett, Mary F. *A Virgin Conceived: Mary and Classical Representatives of Virginity*. Bloomington: Indiana University Press, 2002.

Foster, Richard J. *Celtic Daily Prayer: Prayers and Readings from the Northumbria Community*. San Francisco: HarperSanFrancisco, 2002.

Grassi, Joseph, *Mary, Mother and Disciple*. Wilmington, DE: Michael Glazier, 1988.

Grignion de Montfort, Louis-Marie, Saint. *Traite de la vraie devotion a la sainte vierge*. Paris: Editions Mediaspaul, 1987.

Harvey, Andrew, ed. *The Essential Mystics: The Soul's Journey into Truth*. San Francisco: HarperSanFrancisco, 1996.

———. *Love's Glory: Re-Creations of Rumi*. San Francisco: Balthazar Books, 1996.

———. *The Return of the Mother*. Berkeley, CA: Frog Ltd., 1995.

———. *Son of Man: The Mystical Path to Christ*. New York: Jeremy P. Tacher/Putnam, 1998.

———. *The Way of Passion: A Celebration of Rumi*. Berkeley, CA: Frog Ltd., 1994.

Harvey, Andrew, and Eryk Hanut. *Mary's Vineyard: Daily Meditations, Readings, and Revelations*. Wheaton, IL: Quest Books, 1996.

Henderson, G. Gordon. "The Apparition of Our Lady of Guadalupe: The Image, the Origin of the Pilgrimage." *Marian Studies* 34 (Sept.): 35–47.

Hildegard von Bingen. *Briefwechsel*. Nach den altesten Handschriften ubersetzt und nach den Quellen erlautert von Adelgundis Fuhrkotter OSB. Salzburg: Otto Muller Verlag, 1965.

———. *Der Mensch in der Verantwortung: Das Buch der Lebensverdienste, Liber Vitae Meritorun*. Ubersetzt und erlautert von Heinrich Schipperges. Salzburg: Otto Muller Verlag, 1972.

———. *Symphonia: A Critical Edition of the Symphonia armoniae celestium revelationum*. Translation and commentary by Barbara Newman. Ithaca: Cornell University Press, 1988.

———. *Welt und Mensch, Das Buch: De Operatione Dei*. Ubersezt und erlautert von Heinrich Schipperges. Salzburg: Otto Muller Verlag, 1965.

———. *Wisse die Wege, Scivias*. Ins Deutsche ubertragen und bearbeitet von Maura Bockeler. Salzburg: Otto Muller Verlag, 1954.

Hock, Ronald F., ed. *The Infancy Gospels of James and Thomas*. Santa Rosa, CA: Polebridge Press, 1995.

Hollywood, Amy. *The Soul as Virgin Wife*. Notre Dame, IN: University of Notre Dame Press, 1995.

John Paul II. *Mother of the Church*. Edited by Seamus Byrne. Dublin: Mercier, 1987.

Johnson, Elizabeth. "Marian Devotion in the Western Church." In *Christian Spirituality*. Vol 2, *High Middle Ages and Reformation*, edited by Jill Raitt et al. New York: Crossroad, 1987.

Jones, Alexander, general editor. *The Jerusalem Bible*. Garden City, NY: Doubleday & Company, Inc., 1996.

Julian of Norwich. *Showings*. Translated by Edmund Colledge, O.S.A., and James Walsh, S.J. The Classics of Western Spirituality Series. New York: Paulist Press, 1978.

Khalidi, Tarif, ed. and tr. *The Muslim Jesus: Sayings and Stories in Islamic Literature*. Cambridge, MA: Harvard University Press, 2001.

Kidd, Sue Monk. "A Protestant's Journey Back to Mary." *Anima*, spring, 1989.

————. *The Secret Life of Bees*. New York: Penguin, 2002.

Küng, Hans, and Jurgen Moltmann, eds. *Mary in the Churches*. New York: Seabury, 1983.

Latourette, Kenneth Scott. *A History of Christianity*. Vol I: to AD 1500. New York: Harper and Row, 1975.

Laurentin, René. *Marie Mere de Dieu*. Paris: Desclee, 1984.

————. *Mary's Place in the Church*. London: Burns and Oates, 1964.

Macquarrie, John. *Mary for All Christians*. London: Harper Collins, 1993.

Maloy, Robert M. "The Virgin of the Poor." In *A Woman Clothed with the Sun*. Edited by John J. Delaney, 215–67. Garden City, NY: Doubleday, 1990.

May, Herbert G., and Bruce M. Metzger, eds. *The New Oxford Annotated Bible with the Apocrypha: Revised Standard Version*. New York: Oxford University Press, 1973.

McKenna, Megan. *Mary, Shadow of Grace*. London: Darton, Longman, and Todd, 1995.

McManus, Jim, C.Ss.R *All Generations Will Call Me Blessed*. New York: Crossroad, 1999.

Nasr, Seyyed Hossein. *The Heart of Islam: Enduring Values for Humanity*. San Francisco: HarperSanFrancisco, 2002.

———. *Sufi Essays*. Albany: State University of New York Press, 1973.

Newman, Barbara. *From Virile Woman to WomanChrist: Studies in Medieval Religion and Literature*. Philadelphia: University of Pennsylvania Press, 1995.

———. *Sister of Wisdom: St. Hildegard's Theology of the Feminine*. Berkeley: University of California Press, 1987.

———, ed. *The Voice of the Living Light: Hildegard of Bingen and Her World*. Berkeley: University of California Press, 1998.

Nicholson, R. A. *Studies in Islamic Mysticism*. Cambridge: Cambridge University Press, 1921.

Pelikan, Jaroslav. *Mary Through the Centuries: Her Place in the History of Culture*. New Haven: Yale University Press, 1996.

Potterie, Ignace de la. *Mary in the Mystery of the Covenant*. New York: Alba House, 1992.

Rahner, Karl. *Mary, Mother of the Lord*. London: Catholic Book Club, 1962.

Richardson, Cyril C., ed. *Early Christian Fathers*. New York: Macmillan Publishing Co., Inc., 1970.

Schlink, Basileia. *Mary, Mother of the Lord*. London: Marshall Pickering, 1996.

Six, Jean-Francois. *Thérèsè de Lisieux par elle-meme: L'epreuve et la grace*. Paris: Editions Grasset & Fasquelle, 1997.

Thérèsè de l'Enfant-Jesus et de la Sainte Face, Sainte. Introduction par Guy Gaucher, carme. *Une Course de Geant: Lettres (Edition Integrale)*. Paris: Les Editions du Cerf, 1990.

Warner, Marina. *Alone of All Her Sex*. New York: Alfred Knopf, 1976.

Works Consulted

Luther, Martin. *Luther's Works*. CD-ROM. 55 vols. General editors, Jaroslav Pelikan and Helmut Y. Lehmann. Philadelphia: Fortress Press, 2002.

Migne, J.-P., ed. *Patrologiae cursus completus: series graeca.* 162 vols. Paris: 1857–1866.

———. *Patrologiae cursus completus: series latina.* 221 vols. Paris: 1841–1864.

Meditation / Prayer

The Song of Songs: A Spiritual Commentary
by M. Basil Pennington, OCSO; Illustrations by Phillip Ratner
Follow a path into the Songs that weaves through the author's inspired words
and the evocative drawings of Jewish artist Phillip Ratner—a path that reveals
your own humanity and leads to the deepest delight of your soul.
6 x 9, 160 pp, HC, 14 b/w illus., ISBN 1-59473-004-0 **$19.99**

Women of Color Pray: Voices of Strength, Faith, Healing,
Hope, and Courage *Edited and with Introductions by Christal M. Jackson*
Through these prayers, poetry, lyrics, meditations and affirmations, you will
share in the strong and undeniable connection women of color share with God.
It will challenge you to explore new ways of prayerful expression.
5 x 7¼, 208 pp, Quality PB, ISBN 1-59473-077-6 **$15.99**

The Art of Public Prayer, 2nd Edition: Not for Clergy Only
by Lawrence A. Hoffman 6 x 9, 288 pp, Quality PB, ISBN 1-893361-06-3 **$18.95**

Finding Grace at the Center: The Beginning of Centering Prayer
by M. Basil Pennington, ocso, Thomas Keating, ocso, and Thomas E. Clarke, SJ
5 x 7¼, 112 pp, HC, ISBN 1-893361-69-1 **$14.95**

A Heart of Stillness: A Complete Guide to Learning the Art of Meditation
by David A. Cooper 5½ x 8½, 272 pp, Quality PB, ISBN 1-893361-03-9 **$16.95**

Meditation without Gurus: A Guide to the Heart of Practice
by Clark Strand 5½ x 8½, 192 pp, Quality PB, ISBN 1-893361-93-4 **$16.95**

Prayers to an Evolutionary God *by William Cleary; Afterword by Diarmuid O'Murchu*
6 x 9, 208 pp, HC, ISBN 1-59473-006-7 **$21.99**

Praying with Our Hands: Twenty-One Practices of Embodied Prayer from the
World's Spiritual Traditions *by Jon M. Sweeney; Photographs by Jennifer J. Wilson; Foreword
by Mother Tessa Bielecki; Afterword by Taitetsu Unno, PhD*
8 x 8, 96 pp, 22 duotone photographs, Quality PB, ISBN 1-893361-16-0 **$16.95**

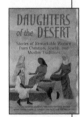

Silence, Simplicity & Solitude: A Complete Guide to Spiritual Retreat at Home
by David A. Cooper 5½ x 8½, 336 pp, Quality PB, ISBN 1-893361-04-7 **$16.95**

Three Gates to Medit ation Practice: A Personal Journey into Sufism, Buddhism,
and Judaism *by David A. Cooper* 5½ x 8½, 240 pp, Quality PB, ISBN 1-893361-22-5 **$16.95**

Women Pray: Voices through the Ages, from Many Faiths, Cultures, and Traditions
Edited and with intros. by Monica Furlong 5 x 7¼, 256 pp, Quality PB, ISBN 1-59473-071-7 **$15.99**;
Deluxe HC with ribbon marker, ISBN 1-893361-25-X **$19.95**

Midrash Fiction

Daughters of the Desert: Tales of Remarkable Women from
Christian, Jewish, and Muslim Traditions *by Claire Rudolf Murphy, Meghan
Nuttall Sayres, Mary Cronk Farrell, Sarah Conover, and Betsy Wharton*
Breathes new life into the old tales of our female ancestors in faith. Chapters reveal
the voices of Sarah, Hagar, Huldah, Esther, Salome, Mary Magdalene, Lydia,
Khadija, Fatima, and many more. Historical fiction ideal for readers of all ages.
5½ x 8½, 192 pp, Quality PB, ISBN 1-59473-106-3 **$14.99**; HC, ISBN 1-893361-72-1 **$19.95**

The Triumph of Eve & Other Subversive Bible Tales
by Matt Biers-Ariel 5½ x 8½, 192 pp, HC, ISBN 1-59473-040-7 **$19.99**

Or phone, fax, mail or e-mail to: SKYLIGHT PATHS Publishing
Sunset Farm Offices, Route 4 • P.O. Box 237 • Woodstock, Vermont 05091
Tel: (802) 457-4000 • Fax: (802) 457-4004 • www.skylightpaths.com
Credit card orders: (800) 962-4544 (8:30AM–5:30PM ET Monday–Friday)
Generous discounts on quantity orders. SATISFACTION GUARANTEED. Prices subject to change.

Sacred Texts—SkyLight Illuminations Series
Andrew Harvey, series editor

Offers today's spiritual seeker an enjoyable entry into the great classic texts of the world's spiritual traditions. Each classic is presented in an accessible translation, with facing pages of guided commentary from experts, giving you the keys you need to understand the history, context, and meaning of the text. This series enables readers of all backgrounds to experience and understand classic spiritual texts directly, and to make them a part of their lives. Andrew Harvey writes the foreword to each volume, an insightful, personal introduction to each classic.

Bhagavad Gita
Annotated & Explained
Translation by Shri Purohit Swami; Annotation by Kendra Crossen Burroughs
"The very best Gita for first-time readers." —Ken Wilber. Millions of people turn daily to India's most beloved holy book, whose universal appeal has made it popular with non-Hindus and Hindus alike. This edition introduces you to the characters, explains references and philosophical terms, shares the interpretations of famous spiritual leaders and scholars, and more.
5½ x 8½, 192 pp, Quality PB, ISBN 1-893361-28-4 **$16.95**

Dhammapada
Annotated & Explained
Translation by Max Müller and revised by Jack Maguire; Annotation by Jack Maguire
The Dhammapada—believed to have been spoken by the Buddha himself over 2,500 years ago—contain most of Buddhism's central teachings. This timeless text concisely and inspirationally portrays the route a person travels as he or she advances toward enlightenment and describes the fundamental role of mental conditioning in making us who we are.
5½ x 8½, 160 pp, b/w photographs, Quality PB, ISBN 1-893361-42-X **$14.95**

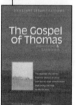

The Gospel of Thomas
Annotated & Explained
Translation and annotation by Stevan Davies
Discovered in 1945, this collection of aphoristic sayings sheds new light on the origins of Christianity and the intriguing figure of Jesus, portraying the Kingdom of God as a present fact about the world, rather than a future promise or future threat.
5½ x 8½, 192 pp, Quality PB, ISBN 1-893361-45-4 **$16.95**

Hasidic Tales
Annotated & Explained
Translation and annotation by Rabbi Rami Shapiro
Introduces the legendary tales of the impassioned Hasidic rabbis, which demonstrate the spiritual power of unabashed joy, offer lessons for leading a holy life, and remind us that the Divine can be found in the everyday.
5½ x 8½, 240 pp, Quality PB, ISBN 1-893361-86-1 **$16.95**

The Hebrew Prophets
Selections Annotated & Explained
Translation and annotation by Rabbi Rami Shapiro
Focuses on the central themes covered by all the Hebrew prophets: moving from ignorance to wisdom, injustice to justice, cruelty to compassion, and despair to joy, and challenges us to engage in justice, kindness, and humility in every aspect of our lives.
5½ x 8½, 224 pp, Quality PB, ISBN 1-59473-037-7 **$16.99**

Sacred Texts—SkyLight Illuminations Series
Andrew Harvey, series editor

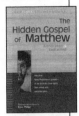

The Hidden Gospel of Matthew: Annotated & Explained
Translation and annotation by Ron Miller
Takes you deep into the text cherished around the world to discover the words and events that have the strongest connection to the historical Jesus. Reveals the underlying story of Matthew, a story that transcends the traditional theme of an atoning death and focuses instead on Jesus's radical call for personal transformation and social change.
5½ x 8½, 272 pp, Quality PB, ISBN 1-59473-038-5 **$16.99**

The Secret Book of John
The Gnostic Gospel—Annotated & Explained
Translation and annotation by Stevan Davies
Introduces the most significant and influential text of the ancient Gnostic religion. This central myth of Gnosticism tells the story of how God fell from perfect Oneness to imprisonment in the material world, and how by knowing our divine nature and our divine origins—that we are one with God—we reverse God's descent and find our salvation.
5½ x 8½, 208 pp, Quality PB, ISBN 1-59473-082-2 **$16.99**

Rumi and Islam: Selections from His Stories, Poems, and Discourses—Annotated & Explained
Translation and annotation by Ibrahim Gamard
Offers a new way of thinking about Rumi's poetry. Focuses on Rumi's place within the Sufi tradition of Islam, providing insight into the mystical side of the religion—one that has love of God at its core and sublime wisdom teachings as its pathways.
5½ x 8½, 240 pp, Quality PB, ISBN 1-59473-002-4 **$15.99**

Selections from the Gospel of Sri Ramakrishna
Annotated & Explained
Translation by Swami Nikhilananda; Annotation by Kendra Crossen Burroughs
The words of India's greatest example of God-consciousness and mystical ecstasy in recent history. Introduces the fascinating world of the Indian mystic and the universal appeal of his message that has inspired millions of devotees for more than a century.
5½ x 8½, 240 pp, b/w photographs, Quality PB, ISBN 1-893361-46-2 **$16.95**

The Way of a Pilgrim: Annotated & Explained
Translation and annotation by Gleb Pokrovsky
This classic of Russian spirituality is the delightful account of one man who sets out to learn the prayer of the heart—also known as the "Jesus prayer"—and how the practice transforms his life.
5½ x 8½, 160 pp, Illus., Quality PB, ISBN 1-893361-31-4 **$14.95**

Zohar: Annotated & Explained
Translation and annotation by Daniel C. Matt
The best-selling author of *The Essential Kabbalah* brings together in one place the most important teachings of the Zohar, the canonical text of Jewish mystical tradition. Guides you step by step through the midrash, mystical fantasy, and Hebrew scripture that make up the Zohar, explaining the inner meanings in facing-page commentary.
5½ x 8½, 176 pp, Quality PB, ISBN 1-893361-51-9 **$15.99**

Children's Spiritual Biography

MULTICULTURAL, NONDENOMINATIONAL, NONSECTARIAN

Ten Amazing People
And How They Changed the World
by Maura D. Shaw; Foreword by Dr. Robert Coles
Full-color illus. by Stephen Marchesi

For ages
7 & up

Black Elk • Dorothy Day • Malcolm X • Mahatma Gandhi • Martin Luther King, Jr. • Mother Teresa • Janusz Korczak • Desmond Tutu • Thich Nhat Hanh • Albert Schweitzer

This vivid, inspirational, and authoritative book will open new possibilities for children by telling the stories of how ten of the past century's greatest leaders changed the world in important ways.

8½ x 11, 48 pp, HC, Full-color illus., ISBN 1-893361-47-0 **$17.95** *For ages 7 & up*

Spiritual Biographies for Young People—For ages 7 and up

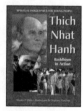
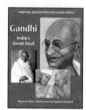
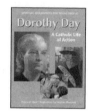
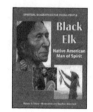

Black Elk: Native American Man of Spirit
by Maura D. Shaw; Full-color illus. by Stephen Marchesi
Through historically accurate illustrations and photos, inspiring age-appropriate activities, and Black Elk's own words, this colorful biography introduces children to a remarkable person who ensured that the traditions and beliefs of his people would not be forgotten.
6¾ x 8¾, 32 pp, HC, Full-color illus., ISBN 1-59473-043-1 **$12.99**

Dorothy Day: A Catholic Life of Action
by Maura D. Shaw; Full-color illus. by Stephen Marchesi
Introduces children to one of the most inspiring women of the twentieth century, a down-to-earth spiritual leader who saw the presence of God in every person she met. Includes practical activities, a timeline, and a list of important words to know.
6¾ x 8¾, 32 pp, HC, Full-color illus., ISBN 1-59473-011-3 **$12.99**

Gandhi: India's Great Soul
by Maura D. Shaw; Full-color illus. by Stephen Marchesi
There are a number of biographies of Gandhi written for young readers, but this is the only one that balances a simple text with illustrations, photographs, and activities that encourage children and adults to talk about how to make changes happen without violence. Introduces children to important concepts of freedom, equality, and justice among people of all backgrounds and religions.
6¾ x 8¾, 32 pp, HC, Full-color illus., ISBN 1-893361-91-8 **$12.95**

Thich Nhat Hanh: Buddhism in Action
by Maura D. Shaw; Full-color illus. by Stephen Marchesi
Warm illustrations, photos, age-appropriate activities, and Thich Nhat Hanh's own poems introduce a great man to children in a way they can understand and enjoy. Includes a list of important Buddhist words to know.
6¾ x 8¾, 32 pp, HC, Full-color illus., ISBN 1-893361-87-X **$12.95**

Spiritual Practice

Divining the Body
Reclaim the Holiness of Your Physical Self *by Jan Phillips*
A practical and inspiring guidebook for connecting the body and soul in spiritual practice. Leads you into a milieu of reverence, mystery, and delight, helping you discover a redeemed sense of self.
8 x 8, 256 pp, Quality PB, ISBN 1-59473-080-6 **$16.99**

Finding Time for the Timeless
Spirituality in the Workweek *by John McQuiston II*
Simple, refreshing stories that provide you with examples of how you can refocus and enrich your daily life using prayer or meditation, ritual, and other forms of spiritual practice. 5½ x 6¼, 208 pp, HC, ISBN 1-59473-035-0 **$17.99**

The Gospel of Thomas: A Guidebook for Spiritual Practice
by Ron Miller; Translations by Stevan Davies
An innovative guide to bring a new spiritual classic into daily life. Offers a way to translate the wisdom of the Gospel of Thomas into daily practice, manifesting in your life the same consciousness revealed in Jesus of Nazareth. Written for readers of all religious backgrounds, this guidebook will help you to apply Jesus's wisdom to your own life and to the world around you.
6 x 9, 160 pp, Quality PB, ISBN 1-59473-047-4 **$14.99**

The Knitting Way: A Guide to Spiritual Self-Discovery
by Linda Skolnik and Janice MacDaniels
Through sharing stories, hands-on explorations, and daily cultivation, Skolnik and MacDaniels help you see beyond the surface of a simple craft in order to discover ways in which nuances of knitting can apply to the larger scheme of life and spirituality. Includes original knitting patterns.
7 x 9, 240 pp, Quality PB, ISBN 1-59473-079-2 **$16.99**

Earth, Water, Fire, and Air: Essential Ways of Connecting to Spirit
by Cait Johnson 6 x 9, 224 pp, HC, ISBN 1-893361-65-9 **$19.95**

Forty Days to Begin a Spiritual Life
Today's Most Inspiring Teachers Help You on Your Way
Edited by Maura Shaw and the Editors at SkyLight Paths; Foreword by Dan Wakefield
7 x 9, 144 pp, Quality PB, ISBN 1-893361-48-9 **$16.95**

Labyrinths from the Outside In
Walking to Spiritual Insight—A Beginner's Guide
by Donna Schaper and Carole Ann Camp
6 x 9, 208 pp, b/w illus. and photographs, Quality PB, ISBN 1-893361-18-7 **$16.95**

Practicing the Sacred Art of Listening: A Guide to Enrich Your Relationships and Kindle Your Spiritual Life—The Listening Center Workshop
by Kay Lindahl 8 x 8, 176 pp, Quality PB, ISBN 1-893361-85-3 **$16.95**

The Sacred Art of Bowing: Preparing to Practice
by Andi Young 5½ x 8½, 128 pp, b/w illus., Quality PB, ISBN 1-893361-82-9 **$14.95**

The Sacred Art of Chant: Preparing to Practice
by Ana Hernandez 5½ x 8½, 192 pp, Quality PB, ISBN 1-59473-036-9 **$15.99**

The Sacred Art of Fasting: Preparing to Practice
by Thomas Ryan, CSP 5½ x 8½, 192 pp, Quality PB, ISBN 1-59473-078-4 **$15.99**

The Sacred Art of Listening: Forty Reflections for Cultivating a Spiritual Practice
by Kay Lindahl; Illustrations by Amy Schnapper
8 x 8, 160 pp, Illus., Quality PB, ISBN 1-893361-44-6 **$16.99**

Sacred Speech: A Practical Guide for Keeping Spirit in Your Speech
by Rev. Donna Schaper 6 x 9, 176 pp, Quality PB, ISBN 1-59473-068-7 **$15.99**;
HC, ISBN 1-893361-74-8 **$21.95**

About SKYLIGHT PATHS Publishing

SkyLight Paths Publishing is creating a place where people of different spiritual traditions come together for challenge and inspiration, a place where we can help each other understand the mystery that lies at the heart of our existence.

Through spirituality, our religious beliefs are increasingly becoming a part of our lives—rather than *apart* from our lives. While many of us may be more interested than ever in spiritual growth, we may be less firmly planted in traditional religion. Yet, we do want to deepen our relationship to the sacred, to learn from our own as well as from other faith traditions, and to practice in new ways.

SkyLight Paths sees both believers and seekers as a community that increasingly transcends traditional boundaries of religion and denomination—people wanting to learn from each other, *walking together, finding the way.*

For your information and convenience, at the back of this book we have provided a list of other SkyLight Paths books you might find interesting and useful. They cover the following subjects:

Buddhism / Zen	Gnosticism	Mysticism
Catholicism	Hinduism /	Poetry
Children's Books	Vedanta	Prayer
Christianity	Inspiration	Religious Etiquette
Comparative	Islam / Sufism	Retirement
Religion	Judaism / Kabbalah /	Spiritual Biography
Current Events	Enneagram	Spiritual Direction
Earth-Based	Meditation	Spirituality
Spirituality	Midrash Fiction	Women's Interest
Global Spiritual	Monasticism	Worship
Perspectives		

Or phone, fax, mail or e-mail to: SKYLIGHT PATHS **Publishing**
Sunset Farm Offices, Route 4 • P.O. Box 237 • Woodstock, Vermont 05091
Tel: (802) 457-4000 • Fax: (802) 457-4004 • www.skylightpaths.com
Credit card orders: (800) 962-4544 (8:30AM–5:30PM ET Monday–Friday)
Generous discounts on quantity orders. SATISFACTION GUARANTEED. Prices subject to change.

**For more information about each book,
visit our website at www.skylightpaths.com**